THE ICE KING

a memoir

Robert Wintner

Wintner, Robert

THE ICE KING / by Robert Wintner

ISBN: 979-8-9865304-1-3

1. Indiana—Ohio River. 2. Family Crisis—Rural Jewish—Memoir. Hustles—Growing Up Poor—Memoir. Printed in the USA

Layout and design: Keith Christie
Cover photo: Leon Wintner, 1940

Contact at RobertWintner.com or Robert Wintner Author on FB.

Twice-Baked Books

$15.00
ISBN 979-8-9865304-1-3
51500>

9 798986 530413

For Perline and Leon Wintner.
And for Brother and Sissy, too.

Also by Robert Wintner

Fiction: *In a Sweet Magnolia Time*
            Lizard Blue
            Whirlaway
            The Modern Outlaws
            Touch of the Unknown Rider
            Reefdog
            Was Is
            Solomon Kursh
            Wintner's Reserve (stories)
            Crux (stories)
            A California Closing
            Homunculus
            The Prophet Pasqual
            Hagan's Trial & Other Stories

Memoir: *1969 and Then Some*
            Brainstorm

Reef Politic in narrative and photo/video:
            Dragon Walk
            Neptune Speaks
            *Reef Libre, An In-Depth Look at Cuban Exceptionalism
                & the Last, Best Reefs in the World*
            Every Fish Tells a Story
            Some Fishes I Have Known

PROLOGUE

I SWEAR TO YOU

. . . I swear to you that . . . I have despised those overly pious people who pray out loud and beat their breasts and bow low and make crazy motions. I have hated those holy ones who talk with God all the time, who pretend to serve Him, and do whatever they want, all in His name! True, you might say that these modern irreligious people nowadays are no better and may even be worse than the old-timers with their false piety. But they're not so revolting. At least they don't pretend to be on speaking terms with God. But there! I'm on the way to Boiberik again.

—Sholom Aleichem, ETERNAL LIFE

I

IN THE BEGINNING

I can only tell you that time doesn't matter, that events get all mixed up, until chronology flies out the window; that most people can't begin to remember what happened in '71 or '73 or '78; that it all boils down to hot and cold.

Stories get lost in time, even the story about the time you die. People won't remember when you died, or which stories you're in or not in, won't remember if the stories happened before you died or after. Go ahead and die, and give them a few years; they'll forget, which makes life suspect, it goes on so easily without you. Does it matter to a story if you were in it or not?

Well, it should, and it does, unless you were a bump on a log. But people mostly forget when. They remember winter or summer, because snow sticks, sweat rolls. But those recollections are more of a feeling, down to the stifling, sweltering, freezing, miserable sting of the thing.

Like summertime in Henderson, Kentucky, right across the bridge over the Ohio River from where I was a kid in Southern Indiana. Hotter 'n a firecracker was the dog-days phrase in that long-gone time, when sayings lost their punch, but people went along, too complacent to step up with new thoughts or words. They wanted to say something but didn't want to offend, and hotter 'n a firecracker was commonly said. It was safer than, say, a hot motherfucker, which could be the saying now, times changing like they have. Nobody said motherfucker when I was a kid, leastwise not nearly so much as now, with social media bringing out the rough side, putting lamebrains and fools on the speaker's podium.

Firecrackers were one reason for heading over the bridge to Kentucky, where just past the south bank of the Ohio River, on both sides of the road, shanty shacks sold triple-cone starbursts, fireball flags, three-foot skyrockets, glory hallelujah heavenly ensembles with multiple reports, jumbo Roman candles, M-80s and cherry bombs and all the baby stuff: ladyfingers, sparklers, snakes, bottle rockets, cracker balls, helicopters, red chasers and buzz bombs. We threw cracker balls in the hallway at school, where the plumbing never worked right because of cherry bombs flushed over the years. Sometimes we divided into armies and made forts to wage bottle rocket wars. I had a model airplane collection that never got past familiarity. Like when my Voodoo Fighter Jet seemed less cool than my new F-89 Scorpion Interceptor, I rigged it with string to a high limb, stuffed the jet ports with firecrackers, and lit her up for a last strafing run—KABLAMMO BLAMMA BLAMMO!

I grew to despise fireworks, but in that time and purpose, obliteration seemed immensely gratifying.

The best of the era was blowing up the *Robert E. Lee* Riverboat Queen with ladyfingers on every deck, in the wheelhouse and at the waterline, which took timing on fuse lengths, so a commando could light 'em up and get to the end of the string tied to the bow to pull it through the tall grass.

For a sweet Saturday interlude, the Riverboat Queen plied the Mississippi, pitching and yawing to joyful annihilation. What oblivion we achieved, me and the *Robert E. Lee*, little gentlemen and ladies, ornate railings and the whole shebang blasting into orbit. I watched, and I still see, no small wonder.

The other reason for heading over the bridge was Dade Park. Horse racing was legal in Kentucky, too. And since the old man knew Mr. Bill Berry, the biggest jockeys' agent at Dade Park, we sometimes got tips on who would win.

It was that simple.

I was eight or nine, focused on foot-long hotdogs on a bed of the only coleslaw in the world worth a damn, so creamy and tart. A foot-long hotdog with the works and a quart of lemonade went for a dollar, more than a sit-down dinner cost then, but the lemonade was squeezed on the spot, and the races out front with a feast in grasp was a winner, especially when Mr. Bill Berry came along and said something like *Friday's Girl*, and life was about to get sweeter still for a few more days. He wouldn't say what race because it was always the next race and always to win, and he never got it wrong.

The old man would laugh when Brother and I asked where is Mr. Billberry, but he'd laugh short, on his own those days, without the biggest jockeys' agent at Dade Park.

Mr. Billberry was biggest because he had the most jockeys. He was also the biggest in size, the first obese person I knew. Fat rolled off him in layers. He had a belly over his belt and another belly under and one more belly under that. Rolls of blubber hung from his arms and off his armpits. Wet, pitted out, he suffered torrential sweat rolling down his chest, into his crotch and down his back to his massive jellied ass. Breathing like a badly tuned engine, he'd wipe his forehead and his chins, waddling our way to tell the old man something like *Gallant Dream . . .*

Now that was hot.

Mr. Billberry maintained the friendship and took an interest. As the biggest jockey agent at Dade, he had his eye on the future. I was a focal point, a prime prospect for jockey school and a stable with a winning record. I tipped in at fifty-three pounds at nine years old, at a size called shrimpy at school, a size that got picked last for any game, touch football to red rover, a size Mr. Billberry called beautiful. "I got my eye on that boy, Leon. The kid looks beautiful. Starve him. Ha!"

Mr. Billberry would hang around eyeballing intensely, talking to the old man about winners and winners' circles and the goddamn Derby for chrissakes.

Brother would whisper in my ear, something like, "How does he reach his pee pee?" We'd giggle insanely till tears ran, unable to stop, even at the risk of a backhand for disrespect or behavior unbecoming a man. But we never got hit for laughing at

Mr. Billberry when the old man was distracted in the vision: me in the roses and the money. He gazed at the future while Brother and I giggled, and the big man rhapsodized on greatness and prosperity. Mr. Billberry practically crooned, envisioning me on a horse at full gallop, I think.

I hit eighty pounds at ten and stayed there two years, and the following summer was scheduled to start my jockey career. Mr. Billberry had talked for years about keeping my weight forward but not too forward, about keeping my weight low, not on my knees, though that's where a jockey's weight appears to be, but lower than that.

Lower than that?

He'd laugh and ruffle my hair, which I hated, and said it looked invisible, but I'd figure it out. He said you only kiss the horse with your knees, let him know you're there, guide him through it.

Kiss him with your knees? And guide him through what?

Through the turns, naturally, and through the changes of pace a winner needs guiding through.

Winning was simple enough for a kid to understand, especially when the old man said Brother and I were good luck. He'd cut us in for ten bucks each after the last race, on the days we saw Mr. Billberry. Few people remember what ten bucks could by for a kid in Southern Indiana in 1957 or '59. On the drive home, the old man would tell us not to worry, because he wouldn't tell Mother we'd won. She'd make us save the dough for college. We decided not to tell Sissy, too; she'd only whine for her share and tell Mother.

Maybe Mother was right. I gained eighteen pounds that spring, and we never saw Mr. Billberry again.

But a kid learns more from burning through ten bucks than he would at college. The old man quit school in seventh grade and was plenty smart. He couldn't make a deal stick, and he was up next to some big ones, but that had more to do with luck. Just like at the track, either Mr. Billberry was there, or he wasn't.

I think it was diamonds that came after working the track, after I gained weight and Mr. Billberry disappeared from our fortunes. I still came in under a hundred pounds, but most good jockeys tip in around ninety-two. I was eleven or twelve and ninety-eight already, way smaller than average but too big for a future at Dade Park. The old man took it in stride, like a man has to do. He picked himself up, dusted off and kept on going. That's what makes him a man, or a woman these days.

Shrimpy size felt like first hard luck, and then I started growing. He saw it as strike two but liked my spunk and spirit, and we kept after it after two solid knockdowns. He called me the toughest one of all. But I wasn't. I was only a small kid willing to go, out and about, running errands, making deliveries and pick-ups, tending to business, drinks and lunch around town. Brother and Sissy wouldn't go. Brother got bored. Sissy was busy.

Every day had errands around town. He had a lull when I gained weight and ended dreams of jockey glory. He'd glance over now and then, maybe hoping I'd dropped the twenty pounds to get back on course. He got over it and didn't bear a grudge. He picked up a line of diamonds from New York to sell in Southern Indiana clubs. I tagged along, unlikely places like the Trocadero, just off the road toward Henderson, isolated and remote in deep foliage, just off a two-lane secondary that, in those days, was primary. Too big for a cabin in the woods, it seemed nondescript, except for the neon sign and gravel parking area.

Inside, guys in suits, brown or gray, and matching hats drank highballs and played cards in smoky rooms from midday to way late. Women drifted, soft and slinky, curling a tail around a man's calf and purring alongside, for luck. Every man needed some, and every woman hoped she had it to give. They moved in a choreography, those women, like women in the movies of the time, black and white. The men played cool and aloof, steeled for action. The winners among them could show success on their fingers with diamonds set in gold. The old man moved easily in that crowd, not so cool and never aloof, drifting and drinking, playing a hand, socializing, and when the time was right, pulling the folded tissue from a pocket to show his wares. He peddled big rocks, a carat or two or three, and sold them cheap compared to retail, if a man was lucky and could pay cash.

Sometimes he'd unfold on a game table, unwrap a dozen little sparklers and watch the hard-edge players pluck every diamond from the tissue for scrutiny. They'd nod and murmur on clarity and color, one or two putting a rock in a pocket. They all settled up without being asked. I doubted that the old man had backhanded them upside the head for being snotnosed punks or yelled at them to turn off the lights for chrissake; goddamn money does not grow on trees.

But they knew he could.

Diamonds, luck and cash made for saucy times. When violence simmered, the old man just stood up. That calmed things down, and he never had to pop anybody in the nose, not for another few years anyway.

We went east to Cincinnati, way up the Ohio River, closer to its industrial source, where the air was a browner shade of pale, swirling with cinder ash and progress. The gray-brown sky matched the dusty brown below. In ambient brown, dirt tones were the color of light, refracting inward to the soul and saying *hmm, yeah, brown.*

The Championship Rounds seemed a misnomer for a drab brown bar in the belly of the beast. The wood floor fairly matched the bar and stools, all brown, and the elaborate, decrepit bar-back in darker brown highlighted bottles in a vast array. They shimmered on a walk-by, sparkling in reflection of the dangling bulbs overhead, evidence of life.

Nobody read the red-brown labels, didn't need to. The sauce *was* lifeblood to the place, the neighborhood, the region, the state of being, frame of mind and up to the firmament. The sauce kept them coming and going, kept them toasting the Kid, kept them betting in the back room, keeping hope alive.

A kid couldn't comprehend the Champ, as the place was known. Sitting at the bar, pointing bottles in a count, I wondered where these guys were before they got there. Where would they go next? Was I the first kid to sit at that bar? And when would the old man finish, so we could leave? A kid didn't know much at nine or eleven. That stuff wasn't on TV, and grown-ups didn't talk about it in front of kids. I sensed that anybody could get anything, one way or another from someone at the Champ, as long as it was seedy.

Men made bets or peddled diamonds in the back room. In the front room, they drank beer or liquor, some talking low, like something going down, something a kid or a Rotary Clubber shouldn't hear about. Some laid it out. Others listened, nodding slowly, staring dead ahead.

A guy in grimy overalls ate a hamburger that looked dirty brown. A very old guy on last legs looked like he didn't know shit from Shinola, grunting and pointing to the gallon jar on the back counter. Half-full of translucent brown with light-brown scuz, it held a pickled pig's foot, submerged but for a toe pointing up, as if wanting out.

The decrepit guy wobbled like he'd covered too many miles and soaked up too many beatings, his overalls threadbare. He looked good for another ten minutes, unless he'd died ten minutes before and didn't know it. Shuffling sideways, he said, "Gimme one 'em blurp glop snuk mmnegghh, Frank."

Frank plucked and served it in a napkin, single ply. The old guy took it plain in his mitts and gummed it, grunting with satisfaction.

I wanted to ask Frank for a barf bag or a stomach pump but didn't, to avoid the backhand for smartass remarks in those days.

Over the bar, in a gilded frame, the cup—a metal jockstrap in brown with a red star in the center—worn by Kid Roundhouse, welterweight champ of the region, rising in victory to infuse pride in the people, so any man could look up from his liquor and think, *the Kid was one of us, and he could take it on the chin.*

I got parked at the bar while the old man worked the back room. I was nervous at first, especially when a few toughs came in, looked me over and asked what a goddamn kid was doing at the bar. Frank told them who I was and that the old man was in back. They bought me a Kid Manhattan and a short draft beer. They ruffled my hair or slapped my back, getting a kick out of a little kid drinking a beer. They were not lovable bad guys, as seen on TV, but ran a murky gamut, nice to nasty. Those outings also ranged, and I could tell how we made out by the pace and tenor of our exit. Quick and all smiles meant prosperity and sit-down lunch on the way home. Quick with no glances meant walk now, out to the car, eyes down, don't ask. Hanging out for a highball or two was the worst. Sonofabitch was a no-show.

The old man took me as often as I'd go those days. He liked me, liked the company, savored the idea, I think, that our father-son relationship was far from conventional and a hell of a thing. Time spent together was our best shot. He didn't protect my tender eyes and ears, figuring I'd see and hear it sooner or later; so why not wise up sooner?

He still called me lucky, wishful thinking that underscored the great value placed on chance breaking right in those days.

I'd gained weight and lost jockey prospects, killing that season's hope to cure our income slump, even though I was still so little, most people thought I was six or seven when I was eleven. He and Brother were thick, and he yelled to leave me alone when Mother tried force-feeding. "He's the healthiest one in the whole goddamn family!" Small enough to have a complex, I didn't, because I didn't care. Expert at not caring, I blocked those vulnerabilities that can take a kid down and lead to terminal sensitivity, rendering a boy cerebral and sissified.

But a tough kid, no matter the rough language and heavy action, doesn't know that blocking is repressing, and the shit will need processing, also sooner or later.

I discounted physical size in a package deal, along with unusual aspects of life at home. I pulled it off, happier in the woods alone than with a bunch of fruit-face kids playing with balls. I heard adults call my solitude an escape from situations that could measure me or render me deficient. Fuckers, talking about me in the third person, like I couldn't hear and didn't have the wits to comprehend the deficiency they claimed.

I gave them silence, a silence I'd brought home from outings with the dog or the old man, in woodlands, where a boy learns to keep his mouth shut and let things play out. I preferred silence to the chronic din of school or shopping malls or any gathering of people.

When I was eleven, softball at school was routine, no big deal. All the kids played. Most other kids seemed dull with parochial parents, making separation and rejection easy. Those kids were groomed to be the next generation of insurance agents, shoe salesmen, civic-minded dads, boosters, glad-handers and so on. I accepted that. It was the way things were.

Vital differences delineated a unique status, I thought, though others thought them merely strange and apart, marginally acceptable as any oddity. I was quiet, not morose. But attitude was a social standard at that age and factored in choosing teams for softball. Distracted, distant, quiet and small, I was not draft material.

Indifference held strong and served well, deferring to eminent superiority in outdoor skills—that was the real outdoors, in the bush. Expert at stalking the wild salamander, hatching mantis chicks, handling snakes, raising ducks and rabbits, I was most relaxed and at home in a forest. Like Noah, I wanted two of each critter to come stay with me for a while. It's what kids did and shouldn't do anymore, with forests mostly gone. My pressed-leaf collection was phenomenal, each one perfectly mounted, identified and described.

That stuff didn't count on the diamond, where I waited to be picked or defaulted to the last scrub, unpicked. I didn't care, also thinking my softball skills not too bad. I couldn't hit but could find a rubbery posture at the plate. Going goofy with nuance, neither here nor there, up nor down, I could assume a subtle, other body to skew the pitcher's read and alter his rhythm. I drew walks. No glory in walking, but I rounded the bases as often as anybody. But points without glory, without drama, were empty. I didn't push the point. I didn't care, didn't try to be chosen or be perceived as a leader—leadership came with attitude, and while both may be real and tangible, they were not, then and there. They were bogus, framed in bogus values in a bogus social construct. Attitude and leadership assured kids of the grand prize, but was nothing, a piñata that, beaten adequately, spilled cheap candy. I knew what those kids would grow up to, what they would do and talk about. I sensed monumental boredom and drudgery, swinging away at a papier-mâché delusion. I felt grateful for the foresight and still do.

Most of those kids had fathers with jobs, as depicted in textbooks of the day, jobs at banks or companies, agencies or professions, jobs in suits or uniforms, office jobs, jobs that lasted for years. Those kids had an air of propriety, the early antecedent of appropriate. They played softball with confidence in what they would become and how they might hit. That sounds resentful and surely was. But they knew security and certainty in what would come to pass, and their fathers would pay for it. They were winners, on the surface. They believed. I begrudged them the view and the time they wasted, my time. I thought them tedious, without fantasy, without hope.

Lines were drawn, and a child profiling now as I did then could give rise to psychiatric concern.

Everyone got chosen or defaulted to a side, eventually, with a groan, a concession to Christian mercy or Republican liberalism, resigned. Let the game begin.

I got right field, like a weed who grew best there. The action was infield.

One day in right field, contemplating straw grass and which type was good to chew and which was sharp or bitter, and how to take care, though nobody probably took a whiz out there, I got to thinking into the green of the thing. Transmuting spectral and prismatic planes, until green went blue, I went snake-eyed to see inside of seeing . . .

A sound arose, a clamor. I looked up.

Charles Kniednagle stepped to the plate. The biggest boy in sixth grade, too big for his age, Charles was bigger at eleven than I would be at forty. His Gothic suburban family thrived on attitude and leadership, a font of goodness in the area.

Mr. Kniednagle sold billboards, changing the face of the countryside with a power seen as profound. Awesome was still fifty years out. Charles' older brother, a State Trooper, wore his stiff, broadbrim hat, bulging britches, a side gun and a smile of dominance everywhere, protecting everyone and everything from badness. Charles would have been a scrub at my size, or if his father fell into the bottle, or his mother had taken the children and moved yet again to another school district. His severe speech impediment could have thrust him to oblivion. But maybe not. He could hit so well.

Charles Kniednagle had thick, dark hair, swept back, only to dangle again over his perfect forehead. Not to worry; he'd fling it back with a toss of his head before speaking, as he did just then, over the hoots and cheers. Charles took his stance at the plate, grinning his big, dumb grin, and he thrust the tip of the bat toward me. "Ih goihg to right field," he said. Oh, how they howled, his team, my team, the girls, the so-called coach, catcalls displacing all else in the din.

It was a proclamation, as grand as the heavens cleaving for archangels and trumpets, calling attention to the no-glove, nobody scrub in right field who would that day be sacrificed for the greater glory. Humiliation rolled to right field in waves. I was embarrassed for existing, for the numbers and words that sized me up. Yet the exercise became a milestone, best seen on a few years of perspective. A turning point in action and spirit converged. Body followed mind.

In the moment, I existed, yet again solitary and aloof. Taking refuge in a familiar mindset was new, socially speaking, that day rising to it instead of bunkering in it. It felt airy and much improved, even in paradox, uncertain yet knowing at last that failure would be mine, and I didn't care.

Charles Kniednagle dug in with great verve. Sadly, he was not Mighty Casey. We were not in Mudville and Charles would not strike out.

I dropped back and back farther. The pitch was served on a platter. Charles grinned and had a ripple, and sure enough thwacked the living shit outa . . .

For reasons then unknown, with powers stumbled onto or granted, I knew the ball could not be caught. Dropping it would return me instantly to my niche, my bunker, anonymous and unknown. Trajectories were foregone, as Charles had promised. A tumultuous cock-a-doodle-doo would cheer him around third. I would scramble like a klutz to find the ball and throw it weakly, short of second base. The action would be rote. It would be glorious for all else and blessedly brief. A done deal unfolded.

Oddly, the powers within eased. I took it for acceptance and felt it as relaxation, coming to terms in profound measure with profound truth. *Fuck it. It doesn't matter. Who cares?*

Charles' line shot on a low arc over the infield, came on like a meteor, until it changed. It slowed down. I watched and waited as hands went up and fingers wrapped and cradled, easing onto the mad spin of it, soft as power brakes. It stopped. Everything stopped, the hooting, the cheering . . . the catcalls, Charles Kniednagle and time.

I threw it in to the catcher, not in the shower of derision hitherto so certain. Silence reigned. I had caught a Charles-Kniednagle line-drive homer barehanded, like plucking a marshmallow from the sky. Adrenaline cushioned the sting and altered the course of nature. It took a minute for chatter to resume, as if denial and I had ruled briefly, as if a flying saucer had landed on the pitcher's mound and nobody felt too good about dwelling on it.

Charles Kniednagle invited me over the following Saturday. His house and yard smelled of mowed grass, like much of the suburban Midwest in springtime. Big grasshoppers flew out back, near the uncut fields. Some had tissue-paper lining under their wings; never mind. Charles pinched the wings off so they could be his pets. Some had stingers, so he held them tight till they stopped wiggling, sometimes squeezing yellow stuff out both ends. He pulled their legs off and set them on his chest, where he could stroke them with a finger and call them by name.

He chose foolish names for his mutilated pets, like Greeny. "I'll call this wuh Greehy." Charles could not pronounce N or S, saying either as a gaping H.

He showed the magic of a pinched-off leg, squeezing the thigh so the foot flicks up. He loved that action. This and other wonders, Charles Kniednagle shared that Saturday, showing what I'd been missing. His big, white house effused stability, his mother, father and brother perfect players for the set. Not a bad guy, Charles, just a kid like me, reflecting the home atmosphere.

He was merely simple-minded with no other kids around, not so mean and with no attitude.

Looking up from right field in catcalls, I'd caught a bit of glory and saw his humility. I wondered if he invited me over on his own or his parents' suggestion.

I thought about it through adolescence, sustaining my belief that it didn't matter, especially in time, changing like we do.

But it did matter in context, even as volition and earlier meaning became secondary a lifetime later, ten years or so, when the kids had hair down their backs, reefers in their pockets and anarchy in their hearts.

Far from suburbs, leadership and attitude, the world had turned to war in Viet Nam, and to fun as frontline defense. It seemed a most fun time of all, with sex, miles of open road and want for nothing but another high.

One day near dusk, I strolled a street near campus with an utterly open mind, a way of being to serve the way things were. Receptive to a brand-new evening, I was high, feeling good, way under thirty, and *time, time, time was on my side, yes it was.*

Out of the blue going gray and a first little twinkle: "Hey, big boy! 'Ow you doihg?" Charles Kniednagle stepped from a doorway. Just as big but slouching to fit in, he grinned.

Me, too, as we checked each other's scene: bell-bottoms, Goodwill shirts and shoes and much hair between us. We'd taken the same route and came alongside at speed.

Taking a moment to fast-forward from eleven to twenty-one, we made mincemeat of the years with giggles and grins and a radical handshake. He hugged me, as if remembering the greatness we'd shared. Well, it had been nothing for me, a forgettable catch in a forgettable game. But for him! He'd entered the realm of humility and perspective. He swayed, holding me.

In that hug, I felt warmth and gratitude. I'd been a factor in his life. Like two Indians meeting on the vast plains of time, we smoked on it, each plucking a joint from a pocket and giggling like fools at the beautiful reality we'd come to. Moreover, smoking a joint with a childhood pal years later in the heart of the revolution was ultimate affirmation, triumph over attitude and leadership, such as it had been. We lit up, inhaling the great truth, that all before was bullshit, hereby thrown over, good for nothing but a goof.

I wouldn't have minded chatting with Charles for a while, but in a minute, I saw that we hadn't taken the same route. Skinny like a speed freak, his long sleeves buttoned, he showed the symptoms. Turning this way and that, like a thrush in the open, on the lookout, he couldn't stay. We'd landed on a live wire and should split for cover, to stay safe.

Keeping time to an erratic beat, he nodded as we finished the joint in silence, savoring the great span of time and progress, as if a joint ten years later said it all. I thought to ask about his brother, the State Pig, what we called police in the revolution, but didn't. Nor would I ask about the big white house or Mom and Dad, thinking all still there, thinking Charles could go home anytime, if he didn't die first. He ended contemplation putting a long, thin arm around me and pulling me in for another hug. "Far out, Mah. You are wuh stohed gah, Mah. You! . . ." He grinned and leaned back to point at me. "I love you, Mah."

"All right, Charles!" I said, wishing him safe passage through the straits of crystal meth. Why do things play out so strange? He walked away, calling back that he played guitar. Twenty-five years later, I still looked under K in music stores but never found him again.

Life in the late '60s had been unimaginable in the late '50s, like the flying saucer on the pitcher's mound. Who could have known? A childhood of discovery in nature was rediscovered. I'd been right all along. Magic was back, for those who could find it. In both times, a boy could find a place of no place and take refuge. Perspective can be fulfilling, if the parts can fit into place.

Southern Indiana is riddled with lakes that reflect the sun and moon and scheme of things. Lakes defined neighborhoods, the biggest enclaves of best houses surrounding the biggest lakes.

Night blizzards howled in icy sleet, shrill and forlorn as lost souls, and a child could be lured away from the fire. A bonfire on the ice on a bed of dirt shed light in a small radius. We flew into the action, ass and elbow, going for the tin-can puck with maple sticks until teams defined themselves by natural alliance, and goal lines were marked. We went at it from darkness at five-thirty to ten or so with no rests, until all stopped suddenly, when too many kids on one spot triggered the tectonic CRR . . . ACK! We moved slowly out, away from mortality.

I raced deeper into darkness than anyone had been, all the way to the weeping willow at the far shore. What a mess, her wild hair tangled, mouth gaping on lament. Raw fear turned a kid to skate back full speed, lake monsters close behind.

A kid takes a lake for granted, out the back door, rich in bluegill that Mother pan fried with green tomatoes for dinner. We swam to the dock with our ducks, little ducks who came in downy fluff, early spring, who we fed and nurtured to feathers and taught them to swim. And ice in winter.

But the most memorable lake had no houses or people nearby and only one road in, a dead end, for a time. A mile or so from our lake in deep woods, a guy came in with front-end loaders and trucks in a campaign to denude Earth in a four-acre radius. In the center, he dug a crater and filled it with water. Earth was unlimited back then, indestructible, no permits required or for sale. The developer stocked his "lake" with baby catfish and set out to build houses around it, big ranch-style, split level numbers to sell for top dollar on the catfish lure. Those catfish could go a hundred pounds in time. Maybe he planned to call it Catfish Acres. I don't know; a kid doesn't see destruction but feels change and excitement, deferring to grown-up wisdom.

A million baby catfish came in tank trucks for dumping into the crater. Thick as pond sludge, the black cloud could bring a sorry laugh at first glance, for the hard luck befalling the Catfish Acres guy. But on second glance: wait a minute! How could pond sludge fill in so fast on a lake just dug and filled? I butt-slid down the steep bank to avoid a tumble and heading home wet, looking stupid. Close to the water, still as a stump, I watched the undulation flutter on the edges, and a few bits came off and moved out but skittered back. My God: catfish. A kid grows up on realization, and this was epiphany. I ran home to make a net from a coat hanger and a nylon stocking. I look back with reservation; it was so long ago, with nobody saying boo on the end of nature.

Meanwhile, in a single inch, baby catfish have pectoral, lateral, caudal, dorsal, and a few extra fins besides, all perfect and miniature, fluttering magically along the sides and top, lips verily talking in the whiskers, through the jar. They didn't mind little crawdads on the bottom, and a few water plants staked in some shallow gravel made for a great show for a few days, until everyone got too big, the water clouded, the crawdads got eaten, the catfish got sluggish, and I happened to see *The Bridge on the River Kwai* that went on to get Best Movie for 1957. Near the end, Lawrence Olivier, head of the POWs who built the bridge, fought the GI commando trying to blow up the bridge. Olivier threw the knockout punch, as the train chug a chug a chug a chugged on the bridge. He'd won, but he squinted and asked, "Oh, God. What have I done?" He fell on the plunger, blowing the bridge to smithereens, so the train and Jap war machine went chug a kablooey into the River Kwai far below.

It felt like old home week; what had I done? I went to a lake the next day and let everybody go and learned to hate glass-tank confinement and its consequence on gill-breathing friends, multiplying the population of that jar by two point eight billion, the human population of Earth in 1957.

A red-eared snapping turtle could bring tears, but giant snappers went eighteen inches across and twenty-five pounds and could stretch legs and neck to spring three feet in a snap to take a hand in a blink, for a lifetime of regret.

I got one to strike an old piece of bamboo pole, and it hung on for the drag home, a grunt and a struggle for a small kid, but piss and vinegar flowed from early on. I regret that, too, and often wish for a do-over, but the world was still endless, a single lifetime ago.

Uncle Rudy came to pick it up and carry it down to the Inn, where Uncle Izzy supervised production on a week's issue of Izzy's notorious turtle soup, nearly as famous as his clam chowder but not so well known. The turtles lived deep, hard to catch, and clams came in a can.

That giant snapper could snap like lightning. The old man came out and shot it twice in the head and shook his head at the pipsqueak kid and said something about soup. We got the bamboo stick pried free of the death grip, imagining an arm in its place, my arm. Then we had a highball.

Instead of too few friends, he saw independence. He didn't sense antisocial inclination but saw a decisive drive to nature. I wanted out and away, into the unspoiled and unknown. He liked that. Ignoring my limitations, he shored up the life situation with certain advice: "Anyone give you any lip, you pop him in the nose." As cornerman, he knew I could. I knew otherwise but thought I might follow through by-'n-by, once I gained another hundred pounds. Meanwhile, it was good, knowing the old man thought I could like he did, and maybe he'd back me up. He was a professional football player two seasons, 1923 and '24, for the Cleveland Tigers, a farm club not far from the Ohio River.

He tried professional wrestling a few years, two-twenty at five-ten. Big-time wrestling was always fixed, but back then it was less razzmatazz and more rough-and-tumble, the real deal. The wrestlers took a punch every so often, and he could, and he could throw back in blink, sometimes regrettably.

Like the time I went to the grocery with Mother and him on a rare family outing. Pushing sixty, coming off two heart attacks in three years from too much liquor and two packs a day, Pall Mall Straights, he loved fried foods and steaks. The good life was what he made of it, and nobody knew about fatty foods, and back then, cigarettes didn't cause cancer or heart disease. Big Tobacco proved it.

Anyway, he asked the bag boy to carry the groceries out to the car. The bag boy should have done it and kept his mouth shut, because the old man tipped big for favors and didn't ask for more than common courtesy. But the bag boy said sure, mumbling out to the parking lot about old farts, fat and lazy. The old man spun on a dime, quick as Sugar Ray Robinson on a one-two, left jab to the chin, right cross to the jaw.

The bag boy was down and back up, spittin' Chiclets and scrambling for distance, as Mother shrieked her mantra about crazy, crazy, crazy, scurrying for groceries with that mortified look she was good at by then. What a scene: *Still Life from Youth.* Or *Grocery Story Parking Lot Punch-Out Shriekfest.* How about *Kroger Mayhem* or *How Check-Out Chuck Learned Manners?*

The old man shook it off and carried his own goddamn bags, composed in short order. He knew the drill from both sides, and he only hit Brother and me for bad manners, when we had to learn like that poor bag boy had to learn, though we got ours with a backhand or a Socko paddle that blistered our asses.

The rough stuff seemed innate to the world and family he came from. His old man, Joseph, was gentle and soft-spoken, his mother, Haddie, known as gracious. They died long before my time. The family went back a hundred years on two generations in Southern Indiana. Joseph came from Germany, Haddie from Austria, both around 1880. Joe went into wholesale liquor and stayed with it. She stayed home to raise five boys and a girl. He was strong and quiet. She was strong, quiet and socially inclined, if society came to her. Living in the same house forever, without pretense, with manners and poise, they ignored the boys' boisterous shenanigans; that's what boys did.

The boys pursued good times and practical gain, raising hell, until they grew old and died.

The impression left for those born later was general. Details get lost with no forebears around to fill in. The big picture comes out mosaic, with gaps between the pieces but coherent from a distance. The old man played on the street as a kid like Studs Lonigan but different, in a small town on a river.

The big picture gained clarity in glances and comments of grown-ups who'd been around and knew the clan as a formidable force, responsive but stable, like a rock the river flows around.

Five brothers who stuck together made for rough-and-tumble times. They didn't look for it but would surely step up when trouble pierced the family circle. Their code of right and wrong was sometimes wrong but mostly right. Ready for action was a mode of being, even as they aged and calmed. A kid can relate to that and learn who and what he is and where to hang his hat.

I was seven when the old man was fifty-five. He was youngest of the brothers. Izzy was oldest, already sixty-eight or so when he decided to reopen the Steamboat Inn. What a great old place that embodied the spirit of the town, or that part of town, and the Steamboat did okay. Izzy knew the business but shut down for WW II. Business had fallen off, and he was ready for a change, for less work and daily detail.

Twelve years later, when the boys sat around trying to figure out why Izzy shut it down, they laughed, not knowing why. The space had sat empty. So, Uncle Izzy got the old place back up, back to life from the dusty, deserted storefront it had become. He got a window painter to scrape off the whitewash and hand paint fancy frontier lettering, white on black with a gold border arcing the front window, visible for a block:

THE STEAMBOAT INN

Izzy got Formica and chrome tables and chairs and a showcase for deli meats, a lunch counter and bar stools, salt and pepper shakers and napkin holders—the works. The floor got waxed and buffed until it glistened, and the place filled with people who'd lived in town for years, people who loved coming down to the river, where somebody had a line in the water. Society happened along the river, and the Steamboat Inn had catfish stew and coffee, like it used to be. River scent drifted the few paces up from the water, cleaner then, fresh and alive. The

Steamboat filled with people from town in '50s suits and dresses for a happening in a current all its own.

Izzy got Paul to work the kitchen again, and Paul still strikes the same dumb pose he did a hundred times for Brother and me, leaning over, palms up, grinning, with a ham sandwich on each palm. We didn't get ham at home, but the old man said it was okay at the Steamboat. Paul had a white shirt and white pants, white shoes and socks and white hair under his white hat, and he served it up on white bread, so the only color in the shot was flesh pink in his cheeks and the ham, with some dazzle in his grin from the gold caps along the front rows, because Paul was practically one of the boys, having seen heavy action.

And it seemed like most of the action was heavy. Like the day these two guys, who also had restaurant interests downtown, came in and roughed up Izzy. Izzy lost use in his right arm and hand from his stroke but didn't let it get him down. He only smiled when the brothers told Brother and me to rub Izzy's gimp hand for luck. We did, Sundays mostly, when the clan convened at Izzy's house for hog jo, a lazy name for hog jowls, a loathsome, cruel dish and regional favorite, fried with potatoes and eggs. Aunt Vi cooked, a red-haired, freckle-faced woman maybe fifteen years younger than Izzy. Their arrangement was called shacking up, a unique label for a risqué situation, but in the old part of a river town in South Hoosierville, nobody gave a shit. It went on for years, and they never married.

Mother said they didn't marry because Aunt Vi wasn't Jewish, but I doubted that; the old man was married twice before Mother and neither of his first wives were Jewish. Besides that, Uncle Izzy and Aunt Vi were products of the neighborhood and its simple pleasures in quaint old days. I think they didn't give a hoot for social convention. Besides that, nobody thought the old man or his brothers were Jewish, no *oy vay* there.

Vi was sweet and gentle, like Izzy, and stayed with him until he died and stayed in the same house till she died years later.

She stopped hog jo Sundays once Izzy was gone, but one Sunday stands out. Izzy put on his best face, strong in a different, quiet sense, confident that nobody could run him out of business the same month he got back in, not with his brothers around, even if the trouble came from a syndication of trouble that ran on the Ohio River. But he couldn't cover the rough treatment he'd gotten with his usual composure, bruised under one eye, not a shiner exactly, and nobody said boo, till the hog jo was way gone under enough coffee to get the boys jacked up, and one of them asked Izzy if he wanted to talk about it.

Izzy didn't want to talk about it. But he understood practicality and unchangeable currents, like the two that ran in the family and the Ohio River, downstream.

Sammy and Rudy and my old man solved the problem, quick and neat with no doubt. They didn't go to the top but sent a message through the boys who'd brought the message to Izzy, roughed up the messengers in accordance with another phrase of the day: to within an inch of their lives.

It happened downtown with no discretion and considerable noise, the brothers cruising fast on foot into one place and another, asking loud: where? They found the messengers soon enough and dragged their sorry asses outside so they wouldn't make a mess and landed into them like a pack of wolves on two unhappy lambs, kicked the holy living shit out of those guys. Then they got down to indelible imprint, to the consequence of laying hands on Izzy: mayhem.

Broken teeth and bones, blood, piss in pants, fractured faces and, of course, heartfelt sentiment yelled at the top of their lungs. The new message got delivered, with witnesses to help pass the new message along. And witnesses were plentiful, right there on the sidewalk and spilling over the curb into the street, where traffic stopped until the beating was thorough enough to be called complete, and the boys stood there, dumbfounded at their power to dispense the truth.

The old man and Sammy carried guns after that. Rudy was the third best pistol shot in the United States Army in WW I. He said shooting was more sporting then and much harder, with the gun down, then raised and fired, one-handed, no hesitation. And he never minded coming in third, still ahead of a hundred-seventy thousand other guys. When Sammy and the old man got guns, Rudy said, "Ah!"

The guns seemed natural to me, not that the old man or Sammy wanted to shoot anybody; they didn't. They just didn't want any bad guys messing them up.

Paul set a record for ham sandwiches that week, because people love a winner, and down and dirty at street level was how the old man and his brothers knew how to win. It was that simple and the only game they ever won. And because it was the biggest week ever for the old Steamboat Inn, I remember just how much fun the place could be. Izzy hung out up front on a bar stool, keeping the place covered, and he'd look to the back when we walked in, and he'd call out, "Oh, Paul! Take care of the boys, will you?" We became part of the brotherhood then, because Izzy saying it made it official. We headed back to the kitchen where Paul gave us a couple of ham-on-whites.

Brother would become vegetarian for life not too long after that, when we visited a farm over in Grayville, and he had a meaningful talk with a pig.

But sitting out front at the Steamboat counter, we got Izzy's Clam Chowder. Uncle Izzy served it, too, to VIPs like us. Hotter 'n a firecracker with spices and so hot otherwise it could send a boy outside to blow steam like a locomotive on the front window, till it formed up and rolled an inch or two and froze in place. Turning around to the freezing sleet and howlingest storm ever remembered, I breathed steam right back at it. The world was cold as the North Pole that week, and a bellyful of Izzy's

Chowder was a campfire in the snow, radiating waves against the blizzard blowing down River Street.

Uncle Izzy died a few years after that, quiet and peaceful as he'd lived. The Steamboat closed, and gone, too, were hog jo Sundays.

Sammy died a year or two after Izzy, and that broke up the old man worse than ever. Only a year apart, he and Sammy hung out at the Elks Club, drinking and playing pinochle. They lived to fish, hot or cold, wet or dry, fish or no fish didn't make a pinch o' shit difference. They didn't need to ask if an hour or six out at a lake, any lake, might be a good idea. Working a bank, casting for bass from midmorning to sunset was bliss for those guys. I went along and got set up with a cane pole and a bobber, and they made me cook, too; I was so much better than mother at making sandwiches with pimento loaf or boloney or foot-long hot dogs from the hot box—any of that nasty shit she'd never buy. I got it all: enough cream soda to regret, dill pickles, Fudgesicles, potato chips, candy. After lunch, I'd search the bank for frogs, tadpoles, snakes, turtles and baby catfish in the shallows. Unique days of hanging out, eating and drinking on sparse talk, they recollect as one long day.

The only time I saw the old man cry was in the kitchen, taking the call from the hospital, knew it was coming after a week of back and forth, watching Sammy fade. He nodded at the news: Sammy's gone. He didn't hang up but cleared the line and called Rudy, then Harry Metcalfe, who lived on beer and sliced tomatoes with salt and pepper, who went fishing with us now and then and was in the brotherhood, all Irish and dukes up at the first Jew-bait syllable. Oh, we could count on Harry Metcalfe.

The old man called a few guys I never heard of and told them Sammy was gone, with an air of finality that told me, too: an era was over. I remember Sammy with a smile. "Hey, kid, come 'ere," and he'd stuff a couple bucks in my shirt. Sure, I liked him, always in a mood, a good one.

Rudy died a year or so later, also no surprise: so diabetic. He'd lost both legs that year and got cancer. He'd moved to New Orleans the year before, to the V.A. hospital, sick and broke as a man can get.

I don't know if Rudy ever married, but I know he never married Aunt Pat, a blonde woman similar to Aunt Vi, whom he lived with for ages. They had about a '39 Dodge coupe, a creampuff cruiser with showbiz panache, like Rudy. He said he could have made it big but stayed home to open the biggest dance studio in the Midwest. Could he dance?

At six, I saw him in blackface; drop my jaw. Minstrel shows were white guys in blackface and striped suits, straw hats, white gloves and tap shoes. They danced with canes and sang *Mammy, How I love you, How I love you, My dear old Mammy* . . . and so on, until Rudy stepped forward and went wacko on the taps. He got hot, sliding across the stage like butter on a hotcake, bubbles popping in his wake, white-gloved hands flying in downbeat syncopation like rhythmic moths just crazy for the flames. Most minstrel dancers painted big smiles on their blackface. Not Rudy, no need, his face fixed on the dynamic of his calling.

He said the world was his oyster back then, in vaudeville and minstrel days. He could have had New York or Hollywood or anything he wanted. All he had to do was go.

He revealed that past as he fixed my face, age eleven, for the school play, a story about Johann Strauss. I played Strauss Sr., a crotchety old fart who didn't understand his son or the glory of showbiz. Rudy puttied me up, gave me wrinkles and gray hair to look very old. He tossed me his cane and took it back to cut off ten inches without a doubt then gave it back. "Now walk. No, no, no." Then he showed me how to walk like a crotchety old fart with a cane.

"So? Why didn't you go?"

"I don't know. I suppose I should have. I just didn't want to leave home."

He stayed home with Pat and played pinochle with the boys, went over the old scores, played his piano and cruised on down to the Steamboat Inn those days Uncle Izzy made his famous chowder. Rudy was different from his brothers, his olive complexion, curly black hair and sharp beak with a hump on the bridge setting him apart with flourish. Brothers and friends called him Dago, because he looked Italian and drank red wine, even as the boys worked up a weekend buzz on Scotch or bourbon.

He said his big mistake in showbiz was not changing his name to Clark Whiting or Lonzo Cassal or something Hollywood like that. He hung on to his name, and everybody got it wrong, saying Winter or Whitner, setting him back. "People won't talk about you, if they can't say your name." He said a showbiz name glows phosphorescent, like Marilyn Monroe or Rhonda Fleming, or it comes on bold like Humphrey Bogart or Rock Hudson.

I thought about that, years later. That makeup session with Rudy was a year or two before all the brothers were gone.

The last time I saw the old man was a Sunday visit about eight months after Mother had filed for divorce. Mother had packed up and moved us across town. He came by and waited in the car for Brother and Sissy and me to come out and go with him for the day, in visitation format back then.

He took us downtown to the cheap hotel where he lived. The room was much cleaner than the hallway. It had a bed, a wardrobe, a table for mixing drinks and a chair. Spartan as Vincent's room but in the artistry of grim retreat, the scene dimmed in soft light, the old man making a small project of fetching ice and glasses for sodas, as if to distract from reality.

The window overlooked an alley. I mixed him a highball and thought liquor made more sense, overlooking that alley. I thought I might have one and pulled the curtain back for a better view.

Sissy said I always messed things up.

Brother wanted more ice in his soda.

We sat around and talked, and he showed us brochures on the aluminum siding he was trying to get excited about selling in Oklahoma. He showed us a racing form he'd been going over for decent prospects that evening. He hung up some pants and straightened his kit, down to a couple bags by then. Then it was time to go home.

We drove home without saying much. He pulled up to the house, and Sissy got out. Brother and I would have followed, but he said, "You boys wait a minute." We figured he'd get sentimental, which wasn't easy for him, but he sometimes did, like signing his letters Daddy, though we never called him Daddy. We sat and waited till Sissy was inside, and he said, "Don't ever change your name."

It's a hell of a request to two brothers, twelve and thirteen. We looked at him. "Why would we change our name?"

"Oh, you know," he said. But we didn't know why boys would change their name, and maybe the idiotic look of childhood made sense for once. "You know, your mother. Her family."

I laughed and said I'd never change my name.

He nodded.

We got out. And that was that, last call, so long, wave goodbye and gone forevermore.

The old man had a nickname from when he fell down as a boy and banged his head on the curb and couldn't remember his name. He guessed maybe it was John. So his big brothers called him John, even after he got his memory back, and those who went way back still called him John.

I read somewhere of the amazing parallels between a person's life and that of the parents. I banged my head in high school wrestling, when I got good at the guillotine. I got cocky and put it on guys a weight class or two bigger. I met my match on a guy five weight classes up, who stood up, laughed and slammed me to the mat. I sat up and didn't know shit and stayed stupid two days in the hospital, where I slept eighteen hours and woke up in the night asking, "What?"

I suppose my wrestling and my old man's wrestling and his pro football were the highlights of athletic prowess in the family.

He survived one more heart attack, but the next one got him. The divorce was final by the time he died, and he'd gone down to Oklahoma on aluminum siding.

I was thirteen already.

The old man's funeral was my first visit to a cemetery, and walking up the grassy lane between the rows, I didn't think much of it, one way or another. Walled in like a park with a bunch of gravestones, the cemetery felt naturally dreary, and the gray day threatened rain. But it wasn't eerie or dramatic like on TV. It was only a place we had to go to and stay for a while, for a ceremony, before we could go home.

But I stopped at Rudy. He'd told me he was third-best pistol shot in the United States Army in 1917, and I read it again on his gravestone. He said he should have changed his name for showbiz but didn't, and there it was. And he was. I hadn't seen him for a long time and sent some childish thoughts his way, before I was urged along. We had to hurry to beat the rain.

The old man's funeral was a somber, perfunctory occasion rather than a somber, sad occasion, what with all the brothers dead and gone and no longer the formidable faction they'd been. Only their sister, Aunt Florence, remained.

The brothers played hard and fought hard and left a trail of harsh recollections. The old man was in the Elks Club for thirty years, but no Elks came to the funeral. They'd kicked him out for popping Dave Begner in the nose and then the jaw, when Dave Begner dropped about a three-carat diamond on the floor at the Elks Club. Dave Begner was rich but wouldn't pay, claiming only glass would break like that. He'd called the old man out, leaving no recourse but to serve up the knuckle sandwich, hot, quick and fresh, as the boys were known to do.

Sammy quit the Elks after that. I didn't want to go there anyway, fuck them and their Thursday-night dollar-buffet that was more and better stuff to eat than we'd had all week.

Most of the old Steamboat crowd was at the funeral, already present in the cemetery. Friends of the family were mostly friends of Mother's, and with the divorce a year past, they didn't come. The divorce began with a ceasefire and became official in a few months. They'd stopped yelling, maybe to gain sense on where the last eighteen years had gone to. The year ended with the old man dead in Oklahoma.

Social pressure in a small town can work like toxic waste. Divorced people back then were stigmatized, unable to succeed in life. Mother let it be known: she'd had no choice. She strove for sympathy and understanding of her effort to save herself and her kids. That and the rain were why we had to hurry, I think, to get on with the new order.

The old man's funeral marked an end to a reality we'd never grasped, to a family disjointed. We would begin that day making our way in the world, Sissy, Brother and I working toward our college educations and success.

Mother knew this in her heart. She told us it would come to pass, whistling in the dark. The family had fallen apart years earlier, and things seemed unchanged. But on that day, we marked time. Everything past became far away, long ago, buried, and the ceremony bore down with expedience, as if beating the weather would help us beat the past and get on with our lives.

It was only us kids and Mother, Aunt Aileen and Uncle Louie, the new rabbi and his wife and a few of Mother's friends.

Aunt Florence had come up from Oklahoma City and aluminum siding. Uncle John couldn't make it; he was so busy with impending success. The old man had died just as they were getting things going. Florence said, "For once, things were working out." She was confused at her last brother's funeral. Mother held her accountable for the way things went. Florence was one of them. She looked like a child lost in a cemetery, surrounded by familiars who couldn't help.

The new rabbi pinned black ribbons to Brother, Sissy and me and cut them with a razor.

Aunt Florence wasn't paying attention and asked the rabbi to cut her blouse and not her sweater, because her sweater was brand new.

Brother and I giggled.

The new rabbi made tsk tsk sounds and said, "Now, boys, this is no time for cutting up." His pun was too juicy to let slide, and Sissy giggled, too.

The general flow felt down and dark, cold and moist, with an overbearing rush to beat the deluge. So it was chop-chop at the funeral parlor and let's get rolling to the cemetery, where Mother, Brother, Sissy and I sat in folding chairs, graveside, by the casket, while the new rabbi spoke about life and death for a few minutes, and it was done. All rise for mourners' *kaddish*.

It seemed odd, rote and foregone. Soon we'd go home. Whatever happened tomorrow would be just as mundane, as if we'd buried solitary strength and independence from social norms. We could move on, beyond values that reflect manhood, and tomorrow we could return to the suburbs. That was tough to figure, and I couldn't, even as we stood to spew a little *kaddish* and be done.

That's when the skinny, stunted kid in front got stuck under roiling dark skies, surrounded by Uncle Izzy, Uncle Sammy, Uncle Rudy and the old man, dirt on the lid already and days of fishing and days at the track and the Steamboat Inn and anything ever dreamed in showbiz—got stuck so bad the sky cleaved and turned *kaddish* into mush, nothing left but a kid verging on manhood and confusion, choked up fit to die and bawling as big as the old man ever was.

That set them off, every last chop-chop, one-two-three, hurry-hurry goddamn one of them; set them off and set them straight, that this was my old man we were laying under; set them off choking and sobbing maybe more for me than for him, and maybe more than me. But that didn't matter, because it all slowed down and started to look, sound and feel like a funeral for chrissake, and not a damn pitstop between gas and groceries.

We moved away from that life and home a few months later. I didn't go back for thirty years.

II

INVASION OF THE IN-LAW PEOPLE

If we hadn't moved, I told Mother for years, I would have studied law at the state university, returned to my birth home and applied my father's gift of gab in a lucrative, professional manner. I would have run for the U.S. Senate and become richer still. The Indiana scenario hit home. She wanted a lawyer.

She'd wanted a doctor but gave up on doctoring when I was only eight or nine, when Tuffy got sick on something foul and nearly croaked. The vet had gathered a fold of Tuffy's skin and stuck in a huge needle on a lead to a plastic bag. All set, he squeezed in a quart of glucose, spreading it around as it swelled under the skin.

I'd faded to a whiter shade of pale and fainted, and a major frame of *Life Comix* is me on the floor, coming to, a nurse dabbing a wet rag on my forehead.

Mother hovered, mumbling prayers for a future of safety and good health. The next frame is her follow-up: "Never mind, you'll be a lawyer."

She clung to lawyerly aspirations until I was ten, then spent a year or two knowing I'd be an engineer. It made sense; I'd continued to get so pale at the sight of blood but then compensated with demolition expertise, blowing up my model airplanes and riverboat queen. She hadn't considered pyromania and low-grade anarchy as symptoms of something else.

In the year between the divorce and funeral, Brother, Sissy and I felt relief. No more yelling. Maybe I missed the noise and blew up my models to feed an inner need. I don't know. I think I was just a kid who enjoyed blowing shit up and making good use of old toys. I could have put my pants on backwards, and Mother would have thought it proof of genius.

When a man on TV said The All-American Soap Box Derby was open to all boys, eleven to fifteen, I realized I was old enough for something at last and announced that I would build a race car and win. She knew I could, having shown such aptitude in engineering. She told everyone: engineering was the field of excellence God had in mind after all.

The Soap Box Derby was more innocent in '60 and '61, about ten years before the little guy who won the whole shebang in Akron, Ohio got busted for cheating. The little guy didn't just cheat, his race car had been wired to an electromagnet hidden in the nose. A button on the top edge of the cockpit cowling was the activator switch. Assuming the position—the race position; everyone else took it in the ass—the little guy lowered his head for a moment of prayer, so vital in the USA, and pressed the button with the front of his helmet.

The starting ramp blocks that held the race cars in place were made of metal. Who knew? When they dropped forward, the little guy's car got launched, getting a jump on every other little guy in the All-American Soap Box Derby Grand Championship. Akron, then, was like Mecca to boys in the USA. The fall from grace was a sign of the times and put everyone in a funk. As a milestone in All-American history, it marked another end of innocence. Walter Cronkite said, "Well, ladies and gentlemen, there is one boy in America unhappier than Richard Nixon this evening, and it's little Jimmy Gronen."

The Akron prosecutor said cheating in the Soap Box Derby felt as bad as the Ivory Snow girl making a blue movie. But Marilyn Chambers developed a career in pornography and didn't seem nearly as perverse.

The big bust on little Jimmy's car led to investigation and conclusion on his build budget, around twenty-thousand dollars, factoring rates for engineers, wind-tunnel testing, a multilayer, custom-epoxy finish, like on the new Corvettes then, and the expert crews to put it all together. Little Jimmy's derby car was cold molded, a professional lay-up by the United States of America Armed Forces, where Jimmy's dad worked. Both Jimmy and his dad really wanted to win.

Walter Cronkite said they'd missed the point. They weren't alone, missing that point in pursuit of another. As with most corruption finally revealed, derby cheating had been rampant for years. I missed many points, but not that one.

The real limit on a Soap Box Derby build when I was a kid was twenty bucks plus twenty bucks more for the official wheels-and-axels kit. Nobody's old man was supposed to arrange wind tunnel tests or cold-mold layups or any of that perfection crap. The old man was allowed to advise on how things are built, as necessary. I was on my own, but how tough could it be?

I didn't have twenty bucks for material or another twenty for wheels and axels, and the old man was out of town by then. I'm certain he would have advised if asked, or least made calls to see what he could find out. We were always resourceful that way. I would have mixed him a highball so he could sit down and tell me what he knew or found out that might be of service. *That* was in compliance with the rules. Some people questioned his moral turpitude over the years, and he was a far cry from the civic club, community guy, booster woohoo (!), gladhanding, grinning, teaching his kid how to cheat.

I had twelve bucks, enough to get started. I paid eight for a two-inch oak floorboard, eighty by fifteen, and four more for the hinges, eyebolts, L-bolts, U-bolts, screws, cables, turnbuckles and stuff, way too much hardware to steal. I stole the plywood from construction sites with Tuffy at night. It was heavy, but we were broke. Tuffy was lookout.

The old man threw in four bucks and promised to be there to see me race.

For six months Tuffy and I spent hours on end in the garage, figuring it out, bolting parts. Brother came out to smoke cigarettes and mess up my stuff. He got fat that year, and smoking cigarettes in the garage was a statement. He didn't give a rat's ass. Sometimes he inhaled.

The racer was a statement, my act of rebellion. I would win the All-American Soap Box Derby like a kid out of nowhere and be famous and rich instead of invisible and poor, and then, you know, I'd be a hero forever, the littlest anarchist, with cheerleaders and tickertape. Brother's smoke didn't help, mixing with sawdust, making smog, and nobody really knew how to nail things together anyway.

Tuffy and I stole a steering wheel from a junkyard Studebaker before learning that nobody used a real steering wheel from a car. Then Official Soap Box Derby Steering Wheel came in the wheel kit.

Sissy said I was a dumb shit.

Wind tunnels, cold molding and lacquer finish? I was cutting Masonite with a handsaw, looking forward to painting the sumbitch with a brush, the tool most often used for painting. I didn't see the fine print under the color, where it said FLAT. What dummy ever wanted dull paint? No big deal, we scored some GLOSS for the second coat with the money from a few nights out stealing soda bottles, good for four cents each then on the deposit.

But the money problem was chronic. Stealing a giant, clunky, Studebaker steering wheel was embarrassing but we didn't care about that. Things came together, kind of, in chronic worry over money, like life. We had no clue where to get the other twenty bucks for wheels, axles and the steering wheel. The build stopped when the steering pulleys got screwed on. No cables could run without the kit. We needed a sponsor.

The old man had gone into retail packaged liquor after diamonds and opened a place next to the 500 PLATOLENE on Diamond Avenue: DIAMOND AVENUE LIQUORS. It looked like a winning set-up. Convenience was the word, concept and lifestyle of the day. So, fill-er-up, check the oil and tires, and while that's underway, why not stroll over to the package store for a bottle or two? It didn't work out, and the divorce was filed as the liquor business ended.

A year later, the 500 PLATOLENE guy still called to see if Mother was okay. We didn't know if she wanted to go out with him, but she understood consequences. The divorce was pending. A tad shrill and off-balance from life gone awry, she reckoned short odds on the old man shooting the 500 PLATOLENE guy, no pending about it. She was wrong. She'd called him crazy for years, sometimes with cause, but I put the touch on the 500 PLATOLENE guy.

Guys call gals, have through the ages and will into the future. 500 PLATOLENE called late afternoon on Fridays, likely pondering another solo weekend. I waited by the phone and hit him up for twenty bucks on this incredible opportunity for national coverage, promising to paint 500 PLATOLENE on both sides, where the TV cameras would home in when I won.

What could he say? No?

A few months later, it was done—gloss black with a big fireball on top and huge decals under the cockpit sides: 500 PLATOLENE, just like on the pumps. I got brass letters for a mailbox post and nailed Comet on both sides in back. It wasn't bad and not too crooked but eons away from wind-tunnel testing, cold molding and multilayer lacquer.

Brother and I took it off the sawhorses a week before the race for a ride down the driveway. Brother pushed to get up more speed to better test the steering and brakes at five miles per hour. Everything was perfect, I thought, or hoped. Frankly, the thing scared me shitless. Brother said we should run it down the street, but no. I didn't want anything to break until absolutely necessary.

Race day brought more and bigger butterflies in my stomach than could be healthy for a kid. Mother, Sissy and Brother watched from the side of the road near the top of Casson Hill. On the starting ramp, assuming the position, I knew as close to nothing as I've ever known. Win and lose didn't mean shit, I just wanted to get to the bottom of that endless goddamn hill.

I'd never heard of a critical racing concept, wheel alignment. And getting to the bottom took on new meaning about ten feet off the ramp. Comet pulled hard left. I pulled hard right to compensate, too hard, because at eleven I knew about driving from what I'd seen in cartoons, so my racing debut was mostly on two wheels, clearing the roadside of pedestrians like Godzilla clomping through downtown.

The old man waited at the bottom. He didn't run out of the way like everyone else but stood there with a thumbs up.

I lost. What a relief.

During the year after my downhill debut, Mother told everyone I'd be going again; I was so obviously gifted with my hands. I built another Soap Box Derby racer, way smarter in year two, knowing exactly where to steal the plywood, saving time not stealing a steering wheel, getting the sponsor money with a phone call, because the 500 PLATOLENE guy hadn't given up.

Moreover, I'd learned on that morning of my first race that The All-American Soap Box Derby is not for boys but for frustrated fathers. Twenty bucks my ass. A kid had two choices: go fiberglass or go home. That shit cost fifty all by itself, with the epoxy resin and cloth, the sandpaper of many grits. Nobody showed all the receipts. What, the official committee would nail your expense sheet for leaving out 80-grit, 120-grit and 150-grit? No. Everybody cheated. All these boys and their fathers showed up with derby cars looking like miniature Maseratis and Jaguars, built for $19.89, with the father saying, "Gosh, we had eleven cents of room left over. Uh ha!" Right. Cheating sonsabitches. That was cool. I was pushing twelve and my paper route made plenty, enough for a racer and a half if I wanted it.

My second racer was sleek, rounded instead of squared, with skull and crossbones on top, engulfed in flames. It felt more radical. I knew about wheel alignment, too, kind of, so I took a few minutes to eyeball the back wheels to make sure they looked pretty damn lined up with the front wheels. The bigger problem, as always, was the weight issue. Boy and car could go two-fifty max, but most of the boys went one-fifty and could get their race cars up to a hundred pounds easy. The first year I didn't care about weight, I only wanted to get it done.

The second year was different. I nailed about thirty pounds of eight-penny nails into the floorboard and then made some enormous fins out of scrap oak, leftover from where I'd cut off the corners of the two-inch oak plank to form the floorboard. That they were simply there, right triangles—perfect for fins— felt like a gift from the race gods.

I loaded all the empty spaces with screws and bolts, technically against the free-floating-object rule, but okay, I thought, with everything jammed in there tighter 'n a gnat's ass. The rig and I still only went two-twenty, but what the hell else could I do? I weighed over ninety by then, which made me part of the weight-rule anachronism: the puniest kids drove the heaviest cars. My race car was a small tank, and I really didn't have time the second year to look too far into brake technology; anybody in my way was going down.

My second Soap Box Derby was my last, in our last summer in Southern Indiana. I drew a first heat against a kid who was already fifteen and a favorite to win the whole thing. He was big, tall, old, manly and with a racer so . . . so right that the run down the hill was a formality. He walked over as the men pushed our racers onto the launch ramp. He looked down at me, ruffled my hair and told me not to worry, just run the best race I could. He said this was his last hurrah, whatever that meant, and after the race, he'd show me everything he knew.

I told him to save it for later, and maybe I'd be happy to show him a few things.

He laughed, and we climbed up, scootched in, assumed the position and heard the ramp blocks drop.

Kerchunk, we hit the pavement, and he was out front right away. But no sooner did I wonder how he did that than I couldn't have cared less; last year I'd only learned about fear; year two was the face of death. Two-twenty and fiberglass went way faster than one-eighty and Masonite. With less rigidity between the body and the floorboard, I felt a wobble.

I cleared the roadside of innocent bystanders, looking like Joe E. Brown yelling, "Whooaahh!" My butthole slammed shut and the whole pile of fiberglass and bolts, nails and screws, oak trees and plywood and official wheels set up a vibration, accelerating to a rumble, threatening delamination and going to terrible visions; I was going over, going airborne, going up in flames.

It wasn't so embarrassing, losing bad to such a favorite and nearly dying. I practically kissed the ground once I got the damn thing to stop—to stop dead from forty miles an hour at three inches above the pavement, hundreds of pounds with no suspension, no airbags. I had the shakes at the bottom, or a half-mile past the bottom, because I followed the instructions on the brakes but never really got the hang of that either, and the back edge of the cockpit put a gash across my back from the pressure of both feet jamming the brake pedal up front.

My fiberglass work needed refining, too, since most of it ended up on my skin during layup in the garage, and what made it onto the racecar had these funky air pockets that swelled up under the epoxy.

The old man waited at the bottom again and came over and picked me up like I was only six or seven and kind of embarrassed me. I expected him to tell me to go pop that fifteen-year-old punk right in the nose, but he didn't. He only said that was the finest thing he ever saw in his whole life.

The kid who beat me went on to win every heat that day, except the last one. He lost to a kid whose racer looked insured, like a little bitty backyard project put together by NASA. But the kid who beat me kept his promise when I called him soon after the race. At fifteen, timed out, he shared a few techniques I'd never dreamed of, stuff he felt certain that a few others knew, except for an iota or two. He said the best start on a racer is on the bottom—turn the floorboard over first thing, sand it glassy smooth and then glass it, sand it and glass it again because no part of a racer causes more friction than the bottom. I pondered bottom friction, as he further advised a flap on the leading edge of the brake hole, to eliminate more friction. Just that easily, I could see no friction on my bottom and knew that I could win next year. The kid who beat me said I could be his legacy. His biggest advice: "Boy, you got to align your wheels." He said he'd show me how, just call him up. Was I excited?

But the old man died six months later, and we moved from Southern Indiana. I remember that kid, a head taller than me and seventy pounds heavier, a regular kid, well-known and admired at his school, a kid who opened up to share with Hoosierville hospitality. I wondered why for a long while but then figured he was just that way.

Meanwhile, Mother got the picture, that engineering was not nearly as promising as the law. A man should study the law, especially a young man as gifted as I appeared to be.

Mother's focus on doctoring or engineering or the law came from her generation's immigrant parents who valued success, legitimacy and pride in a lucrative profession, to better fit near the top, with respect. The drive for money and social standing was simpler then, when doctors and lawyers were assumed intelligent and honorable, unchallenged, upper crust.

Mother hoped that goodness would come to pass and believed that it would, given a chance, and she could improve the odds with mumbled prayers learned from her mother and righteous living. She knew an Ivy League education and professional connections were more likely for a child of stable family and social structure and less likely for child of the free form. She prayed more.

The old man was born in '00, nearly fifty years before me, an age gap that wouldn't seem so great now, but then it did. Adults were much older at younger ages then, with iffy, fatty diets, no regular exercise, more smoking and social drinking. They looked older, men in high-waisted pants with big bellies, women with no muscle tone. He hit sixty when I was a child, and he took solace in fried foods, steaks, highballs, Pall Mall straights, a cowboy movie and another highball or two.

The other kids had fathers half that age, fathers with set careers and civic-minded speech patterns. I preferred our niche and our outings, taking a bookie joint on the river any day over a Rotary meeting. How much better, I thought, hanging out at the track, eating hotdogs, drinking lemonade and beer with guys who had real life written all over them, rather than listen to men in suits talk about the great community we lived in. Oh, I knew them, who they were and what they did. Even at that tender age, I wanted to be an Indian, not a cowboy.

I knew the score; I didn't fault anyone for conforming to type. I just didn't want to hang out with them, much less be like them, compromising imagination and adventurous potential for domestic security. That was tough, dealing with the stability paradox at an early age, wanting a bit of it but fearing the other side of it. We succeeded, I thought, in avoiding the predictable sameness.

Bobby doesn't mix well with others.

Bobby could do better.

My report card often noted social and motivational shortfall. But I did mix well and did better than most, stalking timber rattlers with my Ben Rogers bow and my dog. Far from home, so deep in woodlands the air was tinted green, leaves rustled, a breeze stirred and a great dog read a scent. Decades later, that view remained clear, as if framed and hung on a wall.

I felt luckier than the boys who sat in on civic meetings and learned how to shake hands and heard their fathers speak in platitudes. It felt like superficial goodwill, easily forgotten. A kid knows the difference between puffery and a fresh breeze.

But late summer of '62 marked the fine, thin line between kid time and what came next. A kid begins to see life in wide angles. The old man would have counseled, maybe with a bit more seasoning. But he was gone, leaving Sissy, Brother and me to other perils, namely the in-laws—his in-laws. Many in-laws are more or less agreeable, but the old man had it bad, very bad and then some.

Mother's St. Louis family had taken the age issue to task from the outset, sincerely concerned for the best interests of all parties. The age difference was incidental to having an issue, any issue. They prodded and probed, dissecting to see what was wrong. The Devilment was married to Mother's brother and had a facial palsy or else was stuck on a grin, her headful of teeth beaming in diabolical good cheer, maneuvering for position. Mother called her the Devilment for her chronic debasement of others. Nicknames came suddenly and stuck, for practicality and poignance. Though an in-law technically, the Devilment lacked original blood and couldn't be trusted by Flossie, her son and Mother. Unlike the old man, she strove for the inner sanctum.

Mother's mother, grandmother to Sissy, Brother and me, mother-in-law to the old man, was Flora. He wouldn't call her Flora, much less call her Mother; at two years apart, they disliked and distrusted each other. He called her Flossie, a common nickname for their generation. She didn't like it, so it stuck.

Flossie's son was Mother's brother, greedy, selfish and meanspirited. He'd married the Devilment, a match made in St. Louis, aligning tastes, drives and dental displays.

The Devilment asked, "Isn't it a little late in life for him to get a job?" Interrogation sustained the grin and her laser intention to sizzle the object to grit.

"When do you expect he'll make something of himself?"

"What is it exactly that he did, all those years?"

Many questions crawled from the Devilment's gob, either originally or as repeats to gain favor with Flossie. As a gadabout gossip, the Devilment blabbered nonstop, tortuous as an oscillating fan in hell. She thought it fun, broadcasting the shortcomings of others so everyone could see the problem and join in finding a remedy. The Devilment's most pressing goal, to help Mother, the poor dear. What could be done? The Devilment needed answers.

Flossie and her son would nod and repeat, building their case, asking of the old man, as they would come to ask of me. Flossie, her son and the Devilment bored in, as if steady income for the old man would make a better life for them. They agreed that a backbreaking, brain-killing job a man could hate before turning numb was all that separated the old man from honor, trust, courage under fire and so on. They lamented Mother's woeful lot and sorry odds for improvement.

Mother nodded, sadly, but came to understand their motive, long way around: dominance and positioning for Flossie's dough. Mother took most of her life to see Flossie and her son in truth. "My own mother. My own brother." She would eventually mumble, stuck on disbelief. Alas, reality was a bitch.

The Devilment led the inquisition. Flossie and her son piled on for Mother's own good. Mother dismissed their strange ways. She'd grown up with them, spoke their dialect, knew who they were—until she didn't and knew she never had.

The same questions of purpose and gainful employment were aimed at me, years later. Like the old man, I knew the in-laws from first exposure, from their first doubts in the third person, like I wasn't there and wouldn't hear the problems and challenges sensed.

I would inherit the family business, what the old man ingrained. They framed it as a life of flim-flam and, for all anybody knew, of crime. They called me a wastrel. I called them genetically deficient and spiritless, far from God, in spite of their mumbles and tedious piety. *Zei gezunt*!

Zei gezunt!

Zei gezunt! Commanding each other to be well in a volley of Yiddish Tourette's, they lived apart from coherence, curiosity or substance. A good tale wants sympathy for all characters, but they remained dull, aggressively so, insisting on sameness under them.

On the bright side, like gnats on a dog's ass, the in-laws were easily shooed. The old man ignored them, got them nervous to the point of grinning and glancing. He made me laugh when he couldn't see or hear them, sincerely. Sure, he had the wits to weigh cost against benefit on shutting them up. The ratio was so lopsided that they alone failed to rouse the red-hot temper.

Flossie wailed and moaned, bit her knuckle (not really) and tore her clothing (not really), agonizing over the foul spirit among us. The in-laws viewed Mother's life as catastrophic, a condition of pain and suffering, work and regret. She'd married the old man, and for what?

Unless he was present, and no questions were asked.

He couldn't understand his mother-in-law beyond her vague notions, her rant and rave about jobs, hard work, pain and sacrifice, money and what there must be more of and less of, if anybody hoped to win approval. She assumed that he needed her approval. Nobody cared.

He thought her vile but harmless, except for the noise. He sluffed her off and called her Flossie. She hated that, so it stuck.

Years later, I had a fat, red chicken named Flossie, just as greedy and keen on pecking those nearby but easier to be around, sweeter and not so calculating.

Original Flossie was born in 1898, a peer to the old man chronologically but with no common interests.

Would he, could he, should he keep kosher for Passover, with separate dishes?

The fuck you talkin'?

He cruised both sides of the Ohio River, hustling a buck where he could, and she was just off the boat from Austria, always just off the boat.

She remembered ad nauseum her first words in America: *Gib'm zein inzuts sucre.* Through our youth, Flossie taught the treachery of the world. Give me back my sugar, she demanded on the dock in '05 or '09, because they took the bowl of sugar she'd brought from Austria, unless she stole it from the galley. That seems likely, since her son stole paper towels from public bathrooms and soaps from hotels to get even on room rates. Matchbooks, swizzle sticks, napkins, cheap pens, towels, ashtrays, anything not nailed down was rightfully his, after what they'd charged. His worldview took him to the time of Mercedes.

But back on the boat, years earlier, young Flossie cried for her stolen sugar and stepped foot on America wailing injustice.

Gib'm zein inzuts sucre was original code among the in-laws, conveying in public that the *goniffs* and *schnorrers* were present. That would be the thieves and lay-abouts, the no-goodniks, anyone outside immediate blood and sometimes Mother, she so often failed to follow directions. The bastards would steal your sugar in a blink, and if you don't think so, who cares? You're one of them anyway.

Another sad reminder: remember the lady on the streetcar. Flossie once rode a streetcar with her mother. "You take it," she said of the single open seat.

"No, no," Flossie's mother had said. "Don't worry about me. I'll stand up (in the dark, the cold and pain, the toil and sacrifice). You take it."

"No, no, you take it," Flossie had insisted. And so on in selfless urgency, until a big Black woman, a *Schwartze grosse* of all people, took the seat. Which just goes to show: Flossie and her mother had to stand up, because the lady had taken what was theirs from under their noses. Too wrapped up with each other, they lost again to a world waiting to feed.

The lady on the streetcar persisted into the skeletal phase, when Flossie still harped, "Remember the lady on the streetcar!" She pleaded through the ages, lest ye be fucked. She took what she must, because the lady lurked, ready to swoop and steal what she never hurt anybody to get.

We grew up with it, admonished to keep a wary eye. Anxiety went to caricature. We thought Flossie and her spawn were nuts. Brother gave it a name: the curse. We laughed at the truth of it. We had fun. They had creature comfort and a shitty outlook.

Ah, the in-laws. Flossie shrank, as people do, going closer to the bone in spirit, too. Among God-fearing folk, she stood above, where He could see her righteousness. Mumbling prayers first light to bedtime, she ate, made peepee poopoo, looked outside or heard a sneeze, and she prayed.

She tossed a wad of dough into the trash when baking.

I asked why.

She laughed, mumbling the incantation, saying it was for the poor people in Israel.

Looking into the trash, I shook my head.

She stopped laughing, clucked her tongue and hit the doughball with a rolling pin. "Go. Go see what Mommy wants."

On birthdays and holidays, Mother dialed Flossie and called us to the phone quickly, to give thanks for the five-dollar check sent for the occasion. We went along but stopped at the intersection of evolution and inflation, realizing it didn't mean shit. Or did.

Flossie prayed and baked. The combo seemed compulsive, feeding a spiritual need that remained gaunt. But as we grew, Flossie's needs fleshed out. Abeyance should be generational, she thought, assuming the throne of matriarch, she who would bequeath or not. Her son, the Devilment and their spawn revered her, as necessary. When we stopped calling to say thank you, she asked Mother if we had any idea what it took to get those five dollars? Mother laughed short, because we did.

With missionary intolerance, she proclaimed the old man no good, a bad choice, baking through her mantra, filling her bubble with burble. Chronic baking included a hard bread sprinkled with sugar; a Yiddish form of *biscotti* called *komish broit*. We called it cuntish bread and threw it in pitched battles, once safely back home, to avoid the final conniption.

She made *grievens* or *grievenous*: chicken skin and fat melted, with onion bits added and spread on bread for salting. *Oy*.

Reduced chicken fat is *schmaltz*. It oozed on out in the late '50s, on first insight into coronary thrombosis.

Leftover *grievenous* went to the schmaltz jar, in case somebody needed a fix, salted to taste. Fat dripped off the crusts to run down chins and forearms as it greased gullets. Eating fast made for minimal waste and more lead time on chest constrictions. Tradition called for a cold cola to cut the grease and allay the heartburn.

I didn't think Flossie aimed for coronaries. Grandmothers seek a special something, like bacon grease and biscuits. *Grievenous* was merely a Jewish version of a greasy something. I thought her effort honest in that spirit, until years later, when she discounted Mother as a viable person. Discounting Mother came easily to Flossie, when she factored Mother's children, on advice from her son. I still couldn't think she'd meant to induce coronaries, pressing the not-so-goodness upon us. But bad blood gives rise to doubt.

Besides grease, salt and sugary hardpan, Flossie served up pride in her son. He could have been a golden boy, pitching from a major league mound, she said, but he had to get a job when the father died young, and anyway, a man has no time for games.

He struck out on his own to make sales calls on his corner of the world in "the rag business," wholesaling midlevel goods, mostly from Miami. We asked Mother in those early years why he seemed angry at the people he schmoozed on the phone—his customers.

She didn't know. "That's his way, don't worry about it." She shrugged. "Maybe they should have ordered more."

Flossie's son rarely spent time with the old man but seemed anxious when he did. Obsequious and gratuitous, he came on grinning, tail between legs. Onerous and conspicuous, he seemed pathetic. Effusing goodwill, he shared creepy stories of those who tried to beat him, but he beat them first, as if he and the old man had that in common in the wild world, as if two tough guys could bond. The grin went away when the old man died. Goodwill went to ill will, indicating fear and relief at his core.

Mother moved us to St. Louis a few months after the funeral, at the end of the school year. I stomped, yelled and refused. If she made me go, I'd leave forever as soon as I could. I hid out and finally surrendered. What can a kid do at thirteen?

What's the difference between deep woods and suburban sprawl? A boy reared to nature faced suburban angst in cerebral kids who hadn't sensed the green tint. We drove west, from Southern Indiana across Illinois and over the Mississippi, a week before the first day of high school.

On arrival, we went to lunch at Flossie's son's house. The funeral had been six months prior, fresh but no longer raw. We anticipated a meal after a long drive but got ambushed on a premeditated offensive. Flossie's son would lay down the law, the St. Louis law of the new social order. Still disconnected to social norms and bound to a painful worldview, he had a plan. Things were gonna change. He mumbled as much, to prep us or warm us up or something.

Things? Change?

He spoke low in bits and phrases of need in dire terms. He muttered no money and none to be had and out on the street and so on. He spoke of Mother's need, of regret and anger, presumably his, coming to a boil on the *momzers* trying to do him in. He flushed red over the no-goodniks, with a particular bad guy in mind, good riddance, but now this. He paused on labored breathing.

Children often learn that grownups will support them. Grownups know and care. I knew the old man's take on Mother's brother: soft and cheesy, scripted, stereotypical. He'd lamented his tooth-and-nail struggle in the rag jungle, the blood and guts of buy low, sell high. He recalled an old story again, in fragments, a story he'd shared in the past to no avail; nobody listened, nobody else agonized but Flossie.

Julius Glick had tried to beat him out of twelve bucks on a three-hundred-dollar order. He'd given Julius the dazzling grin at that time, and he grinned again in the retelling, as if in the original moment, that day at lunch. The grin was uncertain, as he nodded in affirmation of short-counting Julius eighteen bucks in goods and adding a carrying charge. He blushed on the moral of the story, that Glick never dreamed of dealing with such an operator. Flossie had moaned in the background at that triumph when first told but wasn't there for welcome lunch.

He looked both ways, as if for traffic, slipping into snippets and other morals, until muttering, ". . .crazy bitch . . ." He gazed off and sighed deeply, softly again trying it on for size, "You crazy bitch." Vocal chords gained sparse traction on the whisper.

Did he tremble? Or sweat?

A kid with instincts felt one of the basics kick into play. The invective had remained on file from not so long ago. It wasn't for Mother, though she could light the fuse in no time, nor was it for the Devilment; she was more devious and greedier than crazy. It was for Flossie, flowing in matter-of-fact monotone from the old man, for all to hear, including Flossie's son, who would not respond.

He shook his head on another nervous grin. Bad feelings were common to many men toward mothers-in-law then; a few comedians made it a staple. But this had come as accusation and indictment. It had made a lasting impression.

It had come just after an outing, when Flossie took Brother and me to *shul* on a St. Louis visit. Deep in prayer among fundamentalists, she lost us. At four and five, we walked twelve blocks back to her place, crying when cars honked, as we jaywalked busy streets.

The stage was set, and the play was likely inevitable, resounding on the old man's stone-cold conviction, "You crazy bitch."

Flossie's son had avoided the old man after that, if he could. If he couldn't, he looked sad, like a naughty pup caught chewing a shoe, grinning, tail tucked. Our move to St. Louis gave him his chance to even the score. Life and years provide such chances, and he took it.

The green beans were cold and half cooked, and I wondered, *The fuck is this?*

We'd been around unhinged adults. We knew when to hear and see but not speak: watch out. We knew when be aware closed the gap to beware.

As if on cue, the doorbell rang. "I'll get it!" He got up, strode from the kitchen through the living room to the front foyer. On a flourish of emotion given to movement at last, he swung open the massive front door of the split-level sprawler with two-car garage for the Imperial and the Cadillac.

A startled little boy asked if Dreba could be in a bicycle race. We could hear from the kitchen. Dreba was baby talk for Deborah and stuck for life.

Flossie's son bellowed, for one reason or another. "Oh, a bicycle race! You want Dreba in your bicycle race! You want your race to be the best! So you want Dreba! Yes!"

Dreba, the daughter, was designated to be the first woman president of the United States. At nine, she suffered far worse than participation trophies, showing failures on several levels. Flossie's son often bellowed, "Look at her! Will you just look at her! The first woman president of the United States of America!"

Pale, awkward and uncertain, she accepted the greatness upon her. It was a joke or not, and she screamed bloody murder at anyone ignoring her candidacy, her nomination, her election and magnificent rule.

"It's not a joke! It's not! He promised!" She would run to her room to collapse on her canopied rice bed with goose down comforter, hand-filigreed corner posts and plush mattress. She would kick and cry, "It's not."

Flossie's son would have the cure. "Would you just . . . look at her!" She would bask, eyes darting.

At age six, she went to her baby brother's room at night, pulled him by the hair down the hall to tell Flossie's son and the Devilment, "Biffa not feel good."

It was true. Baby Biffa did not feel good. Biffa was goo goo for Big Fella, distant and slow. Biffa needed help.

Dreba got yelled at. She didn't like it and loved Biffa more gently from then on, introducing Myrtle to Brother and me a few years later. Myrtle was Biffa's dick. Dreba pulled it from his shorts, both of them giggling, wide-eyed and short of breath, as Myrtle went to an inch and a half.

Dreba would deny the Myrtle games by her teen years, when nobody suggested permanent brain damage but called Biffa a late bloomer. "Look at him! Would you just . . . look at him?"

As country cousins, we thought them strange. What the hell; we saw them once a year, and we were kids. It was easy.

But on the day Flossie's son answered the door, taking that Gothic lunch into history, he cried, "Yes!"

The little boy said the bicycle race cost five cents to enter, for muscular dystrophy.

What a perfect cue, so Mother and her children could see the pressure of the world. "Five cents! You knock on my door and talk bicycle race and Dreba. You want it to be the best! And now you want five cents!" Yelling at the treachery abounding, he made his point: "Mr. Bigshot! You think you can steal my money? And get Dreba in your bicycle race? No!"

He slammed the door and came back, very red, twitchier yet but gratified, having proven his case.

Momentum had built to the next point: discipline. He said we were done with that fat old fart, the good-for-nothing, lazy, drunken bum, and times were gonna change, oh boy. He sought to impress our young brains with the branding iron of need. Flossie's son sizzled in bitterness.

The Devilment watched from the other end of the table, nodding like an inquisitor, on the scent of holy truth. The two strange spawn nodded along in consensus, casting the poor cousins to the social class and circumstance of their making. We were foregone, assessed and concluded in advance.

I hovered around a hundred pounds on that day in '62.

Flossie's son was about six feet and one-ninety, so a pop in the nose had its chronic limitations.

Thoughts crumbled in disarray. In-law world rolled over brutally, an avalanche of insult. It did not feel like the best thing for all, as presented those last few months. Nobody wished us well or sympathized. Nobody assured we'd make it with Mother. How could we, given our liabilities and deficits?

Their truth was traumatic, doled wholesale with a short count and a carrying charge. Flossie's son turned things upside down and inside out. Spewing the effluent of his nature, he showed the worst thing for all, the opposite of forest, river and lake, friends and family. Delivered to the suburbs, we got buried in petty neurosis. Flossie's son had feared the old man but called him fat, drunk and worthless, a deadbeat dead at last, thank God, "I should have popped him when I had the chance."

Brother, Sissy and I got stuck in the chasm of disbelief, that he was actually talking about our old man.

I lost my voice, as in a dream, but reaching deep, breaking high and low, I pushed through and let fly: "You never said that to his face, you chickenshit fucker." Eloquence 1, impact 10. I was thirteen. He was late thirties and wanted to beat me, as in beat me up.

In a blink of realization that he could, he lost his shit, rising to lean forward and over my way for a solid backhand to the face, to get things squared away.

Pure instinct kicked in, whether from the spirit internal or the one who lingered; we can only speculate. I pointed the fork at the oncoming forearm, up from the cold, raw beans. It was only self-defense but . . . Bull's-eye! Even a shrimpy kid can vice-grip a fork on a shot of adrenaline. The fork didn't give but pierced flesh, sinking in.

The big prick screamed mayhem.

Ducking under the table was easy for me, and I scrambled for the screen door in back, as he plucked the fork out and pivoted to the stovetop to grab a frying pan and give chase. What could he do? Beat me with a frying pan?

Blood ties broke that day, leaving a bloody mess for decades. The rift would not heal. In time, the lesion grew numb, and numbness served for thirty years, until events culminated, and nature played out.

All parties adapted, except for Mother, who saw reconciliation just around the corner, any corner. Mother valued family above all. Filial devotion was not a choice for her but compulsory. Flossie was dowager queen with a maid in waiting.

Mother couldn't accept demarcation day in '62. She hoped for peace, so both her families could sit together and eat. Pressing the issue for thirty years, she bought birthday cards for Sissy, Brother and me to sign, to send for Flossie's birthday, calling Flossie's son "Uncle," treating his children like they were normal. Mother's press to make nice inflamed the situation. The fork-stabbing and frying-pan chase were the last contact with Flossie's son for a long while. Bad intentions were mutual, but he would age first. For better or worse, I would not forget.

I got a set of weights at fourteen when the wrestling coach advised that I needed more umph to deliver the goods; don't worry about weight gain. I gained weight and got some umph. Revenge seemed a distant planet, and that was good. Longing to get there can drag a man down. I planned compassion for our resolution but suspected that was bullshit, too. I wanted to maim the prick, pardon me, and took solace in knowing that Flossie's son would exact revenge on himself. A mean spirit so petty and weak will plumb its depths to reach for more. That's who he was.

The fork and frying pan made for change. Mother said for years, "You won! You stabbed him with a fork!" I appreciated that view. She recognized my skills, albeit scrawny and with only four tines. But I liked that, too.

"Do you know he'll try to take everything he can?"

The question gave her pause, as if that phantom had already played its trick. She shook her head to shake it off, to avoid more trouble. She said, "Forget it!" She meant for all time. Dream on.

THE ICE KING

"I'll forget it. Until I'm made to remember."

Reconciliation would never happen, but Mother pressed on, as if a family quarrel should simply be forgotten. The Steamboat Inn and feisty brothers, fishing and drinking, show biz and river-town flair flowed sure as the Ohio River through Southern Indiana and me. Flossie's son was something else. He'd made a big impression.

Mother was different from her family, not greedy or hostile, spiritless or sanctimonious. She pointed out the intense drive that "came from your father" and advised growing out of it.

"Why would I want to grow out of that?" That volley got as old as the rest, and we knew the odds, so we let it go. But she wasn't the first to notice, so I agreed to try nice on for size. If it didn't fit, at least we'd know. I was young and willing, and experimentation is good.

But she tried to orchestrate niceties toward her brother, blind to his potential. It felt wrong, not nice. It didn't work.

Mother and the old man counterbalanced on a chronic teeter. She said the way of Flossie would be in our own best interests, based on Flossie's bequeathals. The old man had a bullshit detector that beeped like a D-9 dozer in reverse. Best interests? Did she really think Flossie's son wouldn't commandeer assets? Did she believe that a turd would one day smell sweet?

Flossie had property and money. Mother had misgivings. Duh. She'd already been cut from Flossie's legacy and didn't know it. Oh, she'd find out.

As she pressed for peace over many years, the best response was to change the subject. She couldn't see her mother or brother for what they were any more than she could sympathize with the old man. I asked a few times how she came to marry him. She could only gaze in wonder. "I don't know."

She knew but remained stunned at how things turned out. The old man wined and dined and gave lavish gifts, like the brand new '41 Ford Coupe parked out front with a pink ribbon around it. Pink! Her very fave! What was a girl to do? He was also forty-one and seemingly brand new. At twenty-three, she blushed when anyone asked how it happened. I think she fell into the rough-and-tumble whirl of a family as free as the countryside with the brothers to set things straight. I think she sensed potential in oil fields, greasy derricks pumping the first few bucks that portended millions. Ashland Oil went on to pump billions, but he lost it, four hundred grand short on startup. It was like millions short back then but peanuts compared to what it became.

That's how it happened, like women have fallen for ages on dreams that could come true.

Over the years, Mother pointed out a silver-haired man here, a fat, bald guy there, here an exec, there a doc, all poised and closer to her age, wealthy and established. She'd say, "I could have married him." Wistfully regretting her choice, her luck, her poverty, she thought any of those guys would have given her a stable home with equity and love. A lawn, some shrubs, decent furniture, and a polished social set didn't seem too much to ask. She pointed out men who'd been ready to court her in the fashion of the day, except that . . .

Here came the country, highballing down the highway. The old man said he sometimes drove to St. Louis in the morning to see a guy about some money, drove back to Indiana for a lunch meeting with a guy about some hardware, then back to St. Louis for the seventh, eighth and ninth at Cahokia Downs and spin by Mother's for dinner and drinks, then head back to Indiana, home by midnight. The glory days had a bead on a vast future of vast wealth on oil fields in Southern Illinois. The tests were done, rigs going in, production on the verge, brave new world dead ahead. The old man saw it in the rough and made the moves on the money, manpower and machinery. He got contracts on transport and stood by to close a deal he'd only need one of. Flying high with a young girlfriend just up the road, he drove fast, drank hard and kept the juggle in the air.

I consoled Mother when she saw those soft-spoken, stable men she could have married. "Yes, but then your children would have been dull." That worked, sometimes lighting her eyes to the color and verve her misadventure had spawned. She might nod sanguinely and stipulate that he was good for nothing but her children.

Sometimes solace failed, and she looked forlorn, like a little dullness wouldn't be so bad. She'd signed on, because a girl had no idea the gifts weren't paid for or the oil wouldn't gush, and potential would wisp away like smoke. It was a hoax, the promise of marriage and happiness. She got closed on a bill of goods by one of the best, a guy who wouldn't take no, who dropped to one knee like Errol Flynn, weaving his fingers in supplication, his eyes sincere. He didn't tell her to take this ring or I'll break your goddamn neck. He asked, "Will you marry me?"

Come on: oil wells, new Ford, pink ribbon?

Questions rose early. The old man never had a conventional job, never arrived at a place in the morning to stay eight hours and repeat, every day. He'd been married twice, and though we never knew his other wives, we knew neither was Jewish. They could have been waitresses or schoolteachers. So maybe she factored her comely, stable character as balance in the fantasy that swept her away. She denied that it was ever good, even in the beginning, when money and affection came easier and the good life seemed close at hand. But it was good, and she sparkled yet again, recalling the Trocadero Lounge out on Highway 41, an outpost in the boonies, where men in suits and slinky women were seen, playing cards and enjoying highballs. She came in on Leon Wintner's arm, a beauty at twenty-three, no drinking or slinking required.

"Tell me that wasn't fun."

"It didn't work out."

Mother was old school: get married, have babies and raise them, relax and enjoy, no big deal. The husband goes to the office, gets paid on Friday and so on, happily ever after. Mother soured quick on no money. Money would remain variable, down-trending. Her lament from way back was no money to buy milk for her children. We never drank much milk, so the lament depended on principle.

She never got over the nerve of things, coming up short. The lament continued long after Indiana, when new difficulties arose. But such is life: shit happens, or stuff happens, or magic happens, depending on socioeconomic status and/or stimuli on hand. Mother granted our request at long last, to put a lid on the milk and the money. She'd settled. A few years in St. Louis, and the hardship of single parenthood with three kids eased up. Sissy got engaged. Brother and I began a long line of menial jobs at a buck and a half an hour, to ease the burden and displace much of the fun time of high school.

Six or seven years after Flossie's son chased me with a frying pan, he came through Memphis. Mother was on her second husband then, a match made by Mother's cousins. An honest plumber who worked every day and never drank, he shared his lackluster life, okay by Mother, but would die a few years in at fifty-one from a liver disease and leave her nothing.

Meanwhile, '68 was Viet Nam time, with divisive politics and many casualties. Flossie's son postured rightwing war hawk, twenty-five years after coming home with "shell-shock." He saw no combat. Shell-shock was his official discharge. The syndrome got refined decades later as PTSD (post-traumatic stress disorder). He'd dreaded shells to the point of shock. Uncontrollable anxiety is a challenge but seemed an odd context for war cries down the road, way past draft age.

Mother asked, "What difference does it make?" She, Flossie and the Devilment called it "a terrible, terrible ordeal."

We called him a fake. And a pussy.

Brother and I weren't going to Viet Nam, and that was an issue in '68. Flossie's son had become a hawk to show something or other, or compensate.

He hadn't shrunk yet, still mid-forties when he came through Memphis. Well, he wasn't about to march into the kitchen for a frying pan to pick up the chase. I looked over to check for fork marks on his arm, stretched my neck and rubbed my arm to rub it in. I couldn't see, and he didn't get it. I was twenty and not fully grown but bigger than thirteen, and things got down in a hurry.

Brother and I weren't allowed to smoke joints indoors then, so we shared one out back and came in to catch Rocky and Bullwinkle at five. We had long hair and other fixings of the day, including a heavy buzz for sharing happy hour with a blood enemy.

He got up and changed the channel from Rocky and Bullwinkle to network news of napalm, bombings, body counts and first rumblings of village massacres. He stepped back from the tube, turned to face us, spread his legs and folded his arms. It was a challenge to come change it back to cartoons. He called us bums for not going to war like the rest of America.

We watched the scene like another episode of Rocky and Bullwinkle. His comic book antics were something else to giggle at. We reviewed options and came up with Mother's curlers, so handy on her dresser. Brother got them and did my hair up to look nice for dinner. That unfolded his arms on a sigh of disgust. We'd ruined the war on TV, and he let Mother know, as she came in, of the travesty occurring under her roof.

"Not now," she told him.

Dinner was served before my hair was done, and I really had no choice but to sit down in curlers. I asked Mother if I should use a scarf, like she did when her hair was up but she had to hit the grocery.

She laughed, "Do what you want, but you're not using my scarves."

Brother said he could take the curlers out and hold everything in place with Spray Net.

Mother said, "It's hot. Sit down and eat."

It was soup, and like two guys working the same rig so long they need no cue, we set up a slurp calliope, one slurping as the other exhaled. It was great for a minute, but we lost it, giggling. Mexican dope made for giggles. Those were the days, and I still laugh at slurping soup in synch with Brother, me in curlers, him in Spray Net, trying to out asshole Mother's asshole brother.

Brother pulled a pack of smokes from his shirt and offered me one. He'd stopped smoking in tenth grade but cockroached that pack from the bathroom, where Flossie's son left it. He smoked Newport Menthol 100s to help ease his bowels. Everyone knew this because he told it with a laugh. "It's the only way I can get a good BM!" It wasn't funny.

"Oh, God," I said. "You touched those?"

Mother agreed, grabbing the Newport Menthol 100s, throwing them in the trash and washing her hands. Coming back, she said, "Cut it out now."

We ate in silence, until Flossie's son complained. "You threw away my cigarettes."

Mother slammed her spoon on the table, overwhelmed with conflict.

He laughed, again at nothing funny.

She went to her room.

We got up and left. I fired a joint on the way out, as Brother turned and said, "Now look what you've done."

He ignored us, finishing his soup and Mother's, having to make the most of a bad situation once again. Soup calliope and curlers highlighted our last encounter with Flossie's son for another twenty-five years.

That was about the time I reconnected with a girl I knew in high school.

We met in '63. I was sophomoric, even then. She was fresh, known at school for womanly features. I worked after school at a print shop and weekends as a busboy for a catering company. Her natural swagger offset her square jaw, narrow waist, wide shoulders and back end. She dated juniors and seniors but liked me for standing out, apart from the khaki-pants, button-down preppies. Pegged jeans and superfly shirts with winged collars went best with the falsetto I practiced on the Marvin Gaye songs I needed for my new band. *Now you chicks do agree . . . This ain't the way it's supposed to be . . . Somebody, somewhere . . . Uh tell her it's unfair, even talkin' in my sleep 'cause I haven't seen my baby all week . . . Can I get a wit ness?*

I didn't know what preppy guys talked about, or why they dressed alike. They suffered a sameness, rote and parochial, dull to the point of pain. Catholic school kids wore uniforms but showed spirit. These guys seemed practically morose, terminally bored and self-absorbed. Not all, but Whippet High did not stimulate exchange among social subsets, only sensitivity to class superiority and specific potential.

Equally demanding, the girls seemed aloof, as girls must learn to be, perhaps, but word could spread fast if a football or basketball player got to feel a girl up, as it were. Gossip was fun but long on repetition, short on imagination. Preppy kids aspired to adulthood, hanging between classes in the Smoking Area, relieving stress with nicotine, like their parents. Many drank coffee in volume and said hell, damn and shit in class, more symptoms of maturity to adult levels of neurosis. Melodrama prevailed, reaching for worldly essence in a St. Louis suburb.

I saw it wrong, not as intended. I didn't fit, another challenge then, a satisfaction now. Preppy boys bonded in dress patterns and a deliberately stupid speech pattern. I tried it but couldn't get it. I finally found the wrestling team, where nobody was cool. Some smoked, and nobody cared. Some drank, and nobody cared. Nobody watched the door or talked about who got in trouble or copped a feel. Wrestling wasn't cool but refreshing.

That high school was unique and perfect for some. I was different, removed and unusual. Maybe that's why sweet Sue batted her baby blues, flashed her smile and laughed out loud at crude comments, craving the crosscut, against the grain, dark and often funny. As a spirited pompom girl and unique package, she also stood apart, commiserating with anyone. As different as a St. Louis suburb from south Hoosierville, we could not close the gap. I shot pool at the community center, where the hoods and greasers hung out and left me alone most of the time.

But we talked in the hall, an amusement for her, a novelty, though I could tell she liked me. People love to laugh, but events of recent years had stacked up, taking my wit from dark to dangerous. Word got around on my "bad attitude," a hurtful phrase but an attraction for some girls. Bad attitude seemed more natural than button-down melodrama. Had I caught on to something at last? It felt like style.

I'd been scheduled to start high school in accelerated algebra in Indiana. The divorce, funeral, move, nasty in-laws and dull, preppy boys at the new school changed prospects. Letting go of hopes and aspirations among adults felt like a defense mechanism. Accelerated algebra? Why accelerate? Why algebra?

Indifference carried over to teachers, counselors and life in St. fucking Louis. Like shit through a goose, suggestions for my best interests didn't stay long in the hopper. A pool table was better, looking down some long green, where life simplified to angles. By year two, I was down to remedial geometry, a special class for dimwits. Some had failed other grades. School was good for clarifying, segregating and moving on in the best interests of culling, seeing who would become whom. The woman who taught slowpoke geometry was painfully constrained and knew the source of evil in the world: testosterone. "If the hypotenuse equals the cosign of the two sides of an isosceles triangle, then why can't side C be the shortest distance between points A and B? Anyone?"

Answers seemed more remote than questions. Teach wanted to paste gold stars on foreheads, but the dummies chewed their pencils, wondering how they would ever make it in life.

I didn't want a gold star and said, "Maybe point A doesn't care." The low achievers cracked up. I got sent to the sophomore counselor's office, lucky break; the new wrestling coach loved chewing the fat with the kids, making him great as a coach and a counselor. We talked prospects, who might fail to make weight and who might challenge for varsity, until he asked, "What are you doing here?" I told him Miss Argyle got pissed off because I said a hypotenuse might not care. He laughed short—he got it! And he said, "Bobby, don't do that. Okay?" As noted, great guy and counselor. His words stuck for fifty years and then some.

Meanwhile, word got around; I'd given the lip to Miss Argyle.

Sweet Sue laughed out loud when the principal asked why I was late again, and I told him: Mother made *farfel* and *tzimmes* last night, and he'd be late, too, if he had to take the dump I just took. She laughed through those years of attitude badness, and near the end of Whippet High, she said yes.

Glory got soggy the day before our date. I got a head cold and should have canceled but couldn't be too sure of another shot. I thought she agreed in the first place for lack of a better offer. I suffered first love, irrational and deep. I wanted fleshy contact, like boys do, but not with Sue. Time together seemed unfathomable.

Labored breathing was okay for the movie but bad for the pizza place on the hill. Sniffling, sneezing and red-nosed as a heroic reindeer, I came up short on the check, a bad sign and a sure indicator. She laughed again and plopped a five spot. It worked out, the fever and sniffles effectively preempting the classic teen struggle, hands and elbows.

Striking out instead of reaching second base set us up for fond recollections down the road, when home runs came daily.

Meanwhile, a girl was touched in the heart instead of on the chest, when a boy reined in, head cold notwithstanding. I doubt she suspected hormonal shortfall but felt weak for the sentiment of no-can-do, waiting with respect and so on. Short on cash was endearing at that age, when poverty seemed temporary, and the future was sure to be fabulous.

We corresponded infrequently for three years. We picked up the pace as pen pals, as needs rose through college. She went away to school. I hit the state U, where reefer, co-eds and protests enriched lost time, in refuge from the jungle war. When we met again, she'd filled out. Her father had refused to fund more college; it was such a waste of time and money.

I thought him weak and timid but correct on the college issue. Stiff as a corpse, he made me wonder how she came from him and other mysteries of nature, including his remarriage to a difficult woman who needed more of everything but college for a stepdaughter. He couldn't get permission to pay for it.

About that time, I got arrested in Daytona Beach when Mike Dowd and I got the idea, in mid-Missouri, that we'd sail the Caribbean. Those were the days of going on impulse. We headed south in my Volkswagen van. College was officially over, ending our draft deferment.

Waiting, we strategized response to Selective Service. Males, eighteen to twenty-six, were unemployable except for menial labor, and we wanted out. We could sling hash, pump gas, wash cars and dishes, sweep, mop, dig, pick and steal, waiting for invitations to the jungle war. Or we could join the world of adventure, not shooting strangers but making friends, all the better in the tropics.

We would drive down, sell the van, get jobs on sailboats and sail around. We left in late June, two weeks after graduation. I needed a wisdom tooth pulled, or we wouldn't have waited.

Finally, free as the wind and stoned enough to feel the future upon us, we headed out. At twenty-two with the experience of eighteen, over taught but under educated, we felt free at last and smarter than in the four years prior. We chose high seas over swamps. It felt natural. Let them find us.

We made Daytona late and parked on the beach, as people did. We would see about a boat the next day. It felt good, close to the earth, buying bread, hotdogs, a can of beans and a can opener. Sunset felt like a milestone on the eve of life, real life.

I didn't want any old boat. I wanted character, like the classic rig on *Adventures in Paradise*. I sensed better prospects for intrigue, glamour and starlets on a classic. I didn't say as much; our quest already suffered self-consciousness, so we let it unfold, eating, smoking hash, pondering tomorrow, when we'd sell the van and sign on. That long day ended on plush thoughts and deep sleep to three a.m.

Cops tapping the windows and shaking the van woke us. They got us out, hands up, legs spread, cuffed and jammed into a cruiser. The vans on the beach at sundown were gone. The cops found a hash pipe on the front seat and frothed on the pain pills in my pocket, for my tooth hole.

They hauled us into jail but got depressed by ten, confirming the prescription. Salvaging a tough collar, they changed the charge from illicit painkillers to narcotics paraphernalia: the hash pipe. They laughed, not to worry; college guys were usually out of the swamps at Raiford Prison in three to five. Their assholes could shrink back to near normal after that, unless we acquired the taste.

What a bunch of great guys, apparently sensitized by name calling, not really pigs, just low-paid grunts. They had a list of lawyers, as required by law, and advised a good one, to best avoid the bowlegged jamboree.

Why, this man right here may be the only man in Volusia County who can save you now.

It sounded like a kickback deal. We called.

Maurice Ligner effused hope and cold comfort: "Oh, gee, we gotta get you guys outa there quick." He advised getting comfortable for the weekend in jail, Friday already, and the bondsman couldn't see the judge till Monday. That would work best anyway, giving us time to get the money together. We'd need a thousand each to start.

But we'd used our phone call.

"Don't you worry," Maurice said. "Let me talk to the boys."

Cellmates were cordial, eyeballing up and down but not threatening. Those in for a year or so were trusties who would remain at County. They brought meals and hung out. The trusty leader, a sharp-featured homeboy from Miami, took an interest. Cisco stole cars, robbed gas stations, fenced jewelry and stayed open-minded. Cheerful, on the lookout for new ideas, he seemed optimistic and upbeat by nature, stepping in as counselor and therapist for two suburban white guys. Professor Cisco taught Reality 101, his reality and ours, too. Cisco's cure for jail: H, and he had some, cheap and clean. Well, reasonably priced and fairly pure, it only got stepped on with mush, nothing harmful.

Disappointed, depressed, our sailing adventure on the rocks, we moped. Mike thought the cure was worth a try. "It won't cure us," he said like a college graduate. "But we're out for adventure, and here we are. Consider the experiential aspect. You can't get addicted on one hit."

Cisco had the works and promised the needle was new. AIDS was twelve years out, but his courtesy and etiquette seemed collegial, and suburban white guys did prefer brand new.

"I don't think so," I said. "I think we could die in here."

Mike nodded. "Yes. We could. That makes it rich."

We debated a day and a half and got out Monday morning.

Maurice showed up immediately after brunch in a twelve-hundred-dollar suit with a valise that stayed shut. He looked like Jan Murray, gameshow host, wavy hair plastered back with pomade, and a standup routine to make the cops laugh. We didn't laugh, seeing him play the game, arranging a ride to his office in a cruiser. We were dirty and his Porsche only had two seats.

His office looked shabby, a hovel with no shingle but a sign: *Honest lawyer, one flight up.* Maurice Ligner and the Daytona Beach cops had built a cottage industry, preying on kids and their parents for thousands on petty bullshit far from home, no different than a speed trap, except for hard time at Raiford Prison as their $word of Damocles.

Oh, you don't want to go to prison? We can arrange that.

The first grand got us out of jail and into Maurice's office. The next thousand would ensure innocence, and after Mother told him what a promising genius her son was, he closed on another grand, to expunge the record, to remove the felony charge and the file. A grand was dirt cheap, he said. No law school in America would take a student charged with a felony, he said. Think how much a lawyer can make, he said.

Maurice Ligner's law degree from Okefenokee U. hung askew on the wall in a cheap frame. How much was three grand each in 1970? Maurice's Porsche was nine grand new.

He got us a sleazy motel room. I called Mother from a payphone to tell her not to send any more money. We were out. It was over. We'd be out of Florida in a few hours, once the van got released from impoundment. I told her Maurice Ligner was a *schnorrer*, a *goniff*, a cheat, and I wouldn't be a lawyer.

She said, "You talk like a crazy man. What did you eat?"

"When? What did I eat when?"

"You get that . . . truck or whatever it is and drive it home."

Mother sent her savings to Maurice, never asking about the felony charge. It didn't matter.

I came home defeated, no prospects but the inevitable invitation to the jungle war, where I might meet guys who could become friends for life, such as it was. My future wife pondered life as a waitress, also in St. Louis.

Could we share a place near campus, where she could finish college as I had done? Two could live cheaper than one, and I'd get another shitty job, waiting tables and waiting for my invitation: Greetings . . .

She hung her head and said yes again. We married in '73, or '74, after a few years shacking up.

Meanwhile, her milquetoast father's new wife looked like Victor Mature and seemed sloshed. He'd changed his name from original Jewish to acceptable generic to avoid embarrassment. Victor Mature either didn't know or loved him for it. She drooled Jew jokes. She and the father resented my two failures: Jewish and broke. Slipping the Hebrew National to the young princess didn't help. I wanted to tell him it was greater than anything he could imagine but knew he'd take it the wrong way.

In-laws can be difficult. Still, stepmother was a shock. She blamed social problems on you-know-who. Among personal challenges: fulfillment of personal needs. Frustration eased on liquor, to a point, where offense came naturally to a bad drunk.

Father-in-law and Victor Mature were a set piece, along with their screwball dog, Sparky, a mini-schnauzer, who bounced, barked and shit on the rug. His feet, yap and butthole were nonstop, spring loaded. Sparky's overbreeding was meant to compensate lack of breeding elsewhere. He died young, replaced by another furry pogo stick, also Sparky. "What a cute little guy," father-in-law smiled wanly.

Sue and I had moved to South Carolina, stumbled onto it by chance, and distance from St. Louis made in-laws easier to bear. We split up a few years later, as familiarity overtook romance. Moreover, early twenties kids have no idea who they're about to become.

Years later, that marriage came clear on basic imbalance with regard to sacrifice, chemistry, round pegs banging square holes. Decades later, we exchanged good wishes and no regrets. Beautiful and talented, Sue got stuck in low-income and zero-mobility with a guy who pored over stories every day, a writer. She couldn't relate or believe the effort would pay out. I thought her friends cleaned and pressed, conventional, predictable, nice and dull. She thought mine droll, unkempt, worthless, colorful maybe, and bums, like in high school.

Sue worked for a state park in town, promoting events. She loved a good turnout. I yawned at wholesome fun for the whole family. She paid the bills those days, days I spent on honing an art form. Sue thought I denied reality, then killed time with no-count friends. She was right but came home to a clean house with dinner on the table. Yet she asked, "What did you do today?"

I might have said, "Pages 130 to 142." I might have shared oblique insight on dialogue or flashback. She stopped asking. We knew the score. Like the oil wells of old, my gushers were fictional, my drilling compulsive. We came to the fork politely, unable to sense each other in terms of calling. We parted on lingering fondness.

'78 or '80 already, time felt right for a move.

Mother muttered that at last, I could move home to St. Louis.

"You mean your place, where I can sit on the couch to watch TV and eat two-handed."

"And what's wrong with that?"

"Next thing you know, I'm brain dead and don't know it." She muttered again for a long and healthful life. We volleyed again over home, as a concept. I told her that in childhood, I could be blindfolded, spun around, rolled down a hill and taken for a drive, and I could still point north. Mystical bonds got broken. In St. Louis, I could point to a freeway sign to show the way. I had no bond but her and wouldn't move to St. Louis.

She said she'd buy me a compass, and besides, I never smoked that LSD in childhood. I told her that leaving my birth home was the first step to a life of wandering, that her anxiety over the places I'd lived and moved away from, cutting ties, displacing, disconnecting, lost friends and a wayward path that looked random, began with that first disenfranchisement.

She wouldn't agree but loved the rhetoric. "You know it's not too late." She meant law school, only three short years to a dream come true, her dream. She imagined an exceptional lawyer in expensive suits, silk shirts and ties, a man and a mensch, a page out of *Gentlemen's Quarterly* demonstrating success in life!

Ah, well. I declined the offer. I wouldn't be Mother's mannequin. I told her: the law was a prospect before leaving Indiana. I assured that I didn't mean to make her feel bad, and things usually turn out for the best, which can take years.

She pondered years and the best.

"I could have been lieutenant governor by now." I meant to lighten things up, but the joke hurt. She regretted her kid stealing pop bottles and mop buckets, as necessary, and couldn't see such dire need turning out for the best in any way but law school. I conceded her point, that picking black walnuts for a living after college and seeking adventures at sea would not have come to pass, if we'd stayed in Hoosierville.

She groaned over losses, one way and another.

"I could be at a desk, a big one, mahogany. Preened and polished. Hardly ever saying fuck or shit. I could have been nice, and people would love me for it. But we moved for the best."

Shutting up at last, she pondered error. She wanted success in a brilliant career and recognition from a grateful society. She'd grown weary of waiting. She'd lowered the bar, wanting a move to her place or at least to her town, where I could eat. A lost boy in the cold, cruel world would surely starve. "I don't get it," she finally said "Moving again? Why? A rolling stone gathers no moss. What are you running to?"

I told her some stones want no moss; I'd been wrenched from home and would roam until finding home again.

"You talk like a crazy man."

I could shut her up on might-have-been, like governor of Indiana, reviewing campaign strategies for the soy bean sector, the Corn Belt vote, the live-crickets-and-nightcrawlers faction, the catfish minority and the industrial north.

She got the picture and mourned another loss, and also regretted lost potential on a law partnership with a strange kid in town whose father was rich.

I often asked, "What do you mean by rich?"

Mother would say, "He's a millionaire. A millionaire!"

But the old man often said the kid's father didn't have all that much, and besides, "Bobby's ass'd make that kid a good Sunday face." The kid was odd, but Mother was best friends with his mother, and they agreed that I'd be a good partner for an odd kid with a rich father.

Sure enough, as a lawyer, the kid wore expensive suits, shirts and ties but never looked too good or generated much in billings.

Mother knew, years later, that the kid raked in the moolah, and the rich father backed him up. It was hokum. Yet she regretted the irony, her kids facing hardship with such amazing brainpower on hand. Or some shit.

So many moves, so many miles and to what? On the road again was what, moving away, growing no roots. Heading out on a cockamamie idea that things will be better far from family and friends?

And girls? What about girls? She meant women. We'd all grown older. When would I find a nice (Jewish) girl and settle down like a *mensch*?

Mother wallowed in woe, framing her kids as victims, perennial waifs, sickly, weak, broke and needy. She scoffed at the adventurous spirit, at freedom to dare, to get up and go. Also blind to her mother and brother, she accepted constraint. Neither mean nor self-serving like them, she saw happiness in a living room with a TV and something to eat. Why not?

But no, I had to run. I told her my roots wouldn't grow once I got uprooted.

She'd glaze, recalling hard times and the old man's epithets through the failed marriage: "Why don't you blow yourself up?" Or, "Every goddamn dime I give you, you piss away baking for the whole goddamn town." Or, "Aw, kiss my ass."

She'd had a few toxic combos of her own. "You're a bum! I don't have money for milk!" And so on.

We got riled up on transience. She wanted a show horse with an elegant wardrobe and a packed fridge to prove power. She preached health and well-being but longed for material success in her children; they'd been downtrodden for so long.

I said she wanted it both ways, wanting the world to exalt her second-rate children.

"I never said you were second-rate."

"You don't leave much room for doubt. Your story is based on your poor, pitiful children. I'm way ahead of the game, but who have you told?" I was yelling again; like father, like son.

Hardship had come along for the ride to St. Louis. We still had special lunch on Sunday, with cold cuts, kosher dills, chips and cola, with no more worry about the old man coming home to detonate on the mortgage or the rent three months late and kosher meats at triple the price. Mother kept a kosher home, obeying Flossie's command. Never orthodox or zealous in any way, she demurred. Back in Hoosierville, the old man had gone ballistic. We'd waited for the storm to pass. The cola went flat.

On her own as a single parent, Mother still bought cold cuts, feeling the sting at two hours' pay but calling it small victory, too. And she loved the greasy, salty taste. She thought quality groceries and new clothes each season were the measures of a good life, or the impressions of it at any rate. She saved nothing; why bother? She spent it all on gifts or bakery but mostly on Sissy getting through college.

Sissy got scholarships, but cash was short. Mother saw four years as allotted time to get Sissy's Mrs. Success for Sissy would be as suburban housewife, making grandchildren who would want for nothing. Mother and Sissy were in it together.

We suffered a run of goofy college guys trying to nail Sissy on the couch, late. Finally, Jerry; all approved. He worked hard enough through college to buy a new '65 Poncho 2+2 ragtop with the big block 421 and four on the floor. He'd toss the keys when he wanted us gone, sometimes midafternoon. They married in July, a month after graduation.

What a relief, briefly. Brother discovered liquor and drugs and roamed with night people, a Midwest gothic crowd who got by in other realities. He kept late hours for years, until thirty, when he changed tracks and got a college degree and a series of advance degrees. He'd researched life in the big lab and would share that data with students, on the consequence of choice, this one or that, inner city. Mother called his off years a phase.

I was headed out again, leaving South Carolina for California. Mother worried and wondered when her sons would settle and rise to greatness, after all she'd been through.

"Both a mother and a father," she often said.

Brother parried one year with socks, handkerchiefs and a cheap tie for Father's Day.

Mother didn't let up but pressed for progress on what counted most in life.

I told her I met a girl.

"And?"

"She's a slut but very nice. Her name is Goldstein. Her father owns department stores and needs a son to take over. I think you'll like her."

Mother's blood pressure could spike on department-store dynasty, until the mirage vaporized. Why joke about such things? Her raw lust for retail glory made her reverence for medicine or the law suspect. Then again, by then, she was ready for anything good with cash flow.

Her generation looked up to men of authority, men in scrubs with knives and clamps, men in suits who held their lapels and spoke ponderously, men of big money. She sensed heady action and money in medicine or the law. But retail was the meaning of life, the give and take, the bluff, the raise, the ruse, the disinterest, the walk away, the close, the tease and, my God, the window displays! Merchandizing was in her blood, and her heart went giddyap on a profile: a Jewish girl with no brothers to run the stores. *Okay, she'll be nice. You'll see.*

Veering to politics could avoid further questions or not. "I could have been president of the United States of America. I could have run at any rate."

"I'm glad we moved. They get shot."

"I could have been vice president."

"When will you settle and establish roots?"

"I don't know. Maybe I am a failure."

Failure hit like an ampoule. "No, you're not! You'll get it. When it's time."

"You think so?"

The old man never figured this out, never got past the relentless challenge but duked it out daily.

Truth was: Mother spent every goddamn dime on baking for others. What a nut, and what a cook. She baked and gave. Baking was her gift, and she thought people would reciprocate. This was naive, and she pressed on, seeing no alternative.

She packed lunch in a brown bag for Tuffy and me, for our woodland walks into the great beyond across the street.

Saturday Night at the Movies was a TV phenom in radical departure. Movies at home?

The Saturday extravaganza for kids was ten to five in a theater, two dimes to get in, another dime for popcorn and a nickel for a soda. It began with twenty cartoons and went to Hopalong Cassidy, the Three Stooges, Jungle Jim, Tarzan and Captain Midnight for starters. *Earth Vs. The Flying Saucers*, *Forbidden Planet*, *Thirteen Ghosts*, *The Seventh Voyage of Sinbad* and the rest wrapped things up. Packed with kids, the place screamed bloody murder, popcorn and candy flying, cutting loose from school.

But movies paled next to summer mornings, headed out with Tuffy and lunch in a bag. We met sunrise with full hearts. Out early, we crossed the road and field to the high canopy, following deer paths or instinct. Walking, listening and soaking it up, we quenched a thirst common to kids and dogs. In an hour, we sat on a fallen tree to open the bag on sandwiches, baked chicken, carrot and celery sticks, olives, deviled eggs, chips, pickles, cake and cookies, a dish, water in a jar, two napkins and chewing gum. We felt Mother's presence, as intended.

Lunch in a bag lingers, but that forest is buried like the rest. World population in '59 was three billion. Fewer people made for nobler times.

Tuffy showed more character than most people. He walked mornings a half mile to the bus stop and watched us get on and ride away, sad for a good day wasted. He walked home to nap and walked back to the bus stop at two thirty, to come alive until dark. We worked the streets, selling seeds or greeting cards door-to-door. He ran alongside, afternoons, on my paper route. Sunday mornings began at four a.m., finished by sunrise.

Human population on Earth tripled in sixty years, woodlands got paved, and a boy better have his dog on a leash. Old Mom often asked if I wanted my lunch in a bag. But where would I take it? She was only kidding anyway, I think.

Decades later, Brother visited my island home in the middle of the Pacific. He rode my bike a few miles down a country road and stopped to sit in the green tint. When a cold nose touched his ear, he turned. Tuffy greeted, tail wagging.

After a fervent reunion, he determined to walk the bicycle so Tuffy could follow. But turning briefly to pick it up and turning back, Tuffy was gone. Tuffy would have been thirty-eight that year but died in '68 at fourteen. Tuffy's mother, Beanie, came in '53 but got run over a year later, a week after having pups that got bottle fed and hand groomed. We shrieked when they peed on us. Tuffy, too. I was five.

I told Brother it was acid flashback.

He said, "Yeah, but it was real."

I couldn't argue. When Brother went home, I packed lunch in a bag . . . and ate it in the kitchen. What? Head out on my bike to look for my childhood dog? Still, that sandwich recalled a few old dreams long lost.

Days of youth and natural wonder gave way in a few years to the jungle war, as seen on TV. Avoiding the war required college—four years of dope, psychedelics and coeds, a waste of time but for the fun, fun, fun and joy at hand. Acid flashback is great if available.

My first job application, post-grad, had a blank to fill in: Education: _____. I wrote: *the woods across the street with my dog*. I didn't get the job, didn't want it if I had to lie.

Meanwhile, adolescence had occurred in St. Louis. We fought like siblings. Sissy screamed for space and quiet. Brother got fat, over two hundred pounds at fourteen, and looked bigger when I tipped in at a hundred, at thirteen. Sissy thought Mother had failed, winding up like she did. Brother got high.

Sissy hated having me around, small but in the way, playing the radio too loud for college homework.

I ignored her, lifting barbells with little grunts and squeals in the gap between the cot and the dresser, now and then chirping that she could go fuck herself.

She'd storm out, or we'd fight.

We fought over what record would go on the hi-fi. Sissy had a new LP by a tone-deaf nerd who sang about beatnik stuff and called himself Dylan, another Jewish kid from the suburbs trying to gain attention.

I told her that guy was a *schmendrik*, and I needed to practice with the Ronnettes. . . *Be my, be my bay-by. My wuun and only bay-by . . . Wha, wha, wha, wha . . .*

Sissy yelled that I was an accident, a mistake, and one day spit it out: bad diaphragm.

I asked Mother, what's a diaphragm and what did Sissy mean?

Mother shrugged, "Why worry about it now?"

"How did Sissy know about the bad diaphragm?"

Mother said, "How do I know how she knows?" Mother made small efforts after that to let me know it happened for the best; more cookies or baked chicken weren't new; she'd always force fed the little one, but the solicitous gesture gained purpose.

Not to worry. I liked accidental. A low-odds individual had cleared the first hurdle and kept on coming, unstoppable.

Sissy said I was warped.

I think she bore a grudge from a few years earlier, when I called her a whore during a fight. Sissy was in high school, striving for cool maturity but coming home to a zoo. She told Mother I'd called her a whore.

Mother told the old man.

He asked if I knew what a whore was.

I was ten. I said sure: Sissy's a whore.

We went for a drive in the '57 DeSoto, black and white two-tone, red interior and push-button drive and three tail-gun lights stacked on either side, on back of the rocket fins. The old man gave Brother and me the scoop on men and women, and what men did with their dicks. Most unbelievable, and we didn't believe it, was the idea that men liked doing it, liked it so much, well, that's where the whores came in. He didn't get around to women liking it. For one thing, that seemed worse than unbelievable. That seemed crazy. For another thing, it was only '57, and women didn't like it yet.

Brother and I spent the standard week staring at married people and giggling.

Sissy looked smug. She'd known for years.

I told her softly, she was still a whore.

She screamed and told.

I denied everything.

When Sissy grew long fingernails a few years later in St. Louis, she dug them into our forearms; we were such shits in need of scarring. Kids at school thought we had a disease that caused cuts and scabs on our forearms.

The rash went into remission the year I gained fifteen pounds and clocked Sissy. We stopped fighting soon after and eventually came to help each other.

Mother remarried in '68 and moved to Memphis.

That was college time, year two, and I got a summer job at a match factory for a dollar ninety-two an hour, big money that would set me up for a year. But I got an ulcer. Too much repression got me at twenty. Too much denial of the world on top, too much struggle staying afloat, too much worry, too little money, no fun. I moved in with Sissy and Jerry and ate pablum till the pain eased up. I quit the match factory; better to stay poor. Sissy ditched the bullshit. It was only a thing of the past and fell away. Fuck matches. The pain went away, too. Strong and young again, dream intact, I hit the road like I should have instead of giving in to getting ahead. I got ahead, heading out on the next leg of the trip some people have to take.

Sissy and Jerry moved to Alabama to start having babies.

Mother was forty-four, getting old already. Still loyal to Flossie and Flossie's son and regretting the rift, she urged us to "do the right thing." She thought the rift would go away, and her families could reunite in the struggle against the world. The struggle raged in Mother's other family, Flossie's son valiantly beating the bastards coming at him, spewing tales of woe, supporting his family and hers. That is, Mother worked for him, causing another hardship: he had to pay her.

Flossie clicked her tongue and mumbled prayers, invoking God to help her son against the bastards, beseeching more money to support so many people.

Still in the rag business, Flossie's son sold cheap clothing presented as quality goods. Mother was secretary and frontline defender for sixty bucks a week. She didn't complain, except when the Devilment swept in like the Queen of Sheba or Dinah Shore or Sister Woman. The Devilment was unique but not like an actress or TV hostess or Queen.

Face chiseled, eyes popping, she moved to within inches, as if to inhale the victim's soul. Did she practice that at home? *Mirror, mirror, on the wall, who is most socially connected of all?* Mother and Flossie hated the Devilment. Flossie's son called their loathing another hardship. Didn't he have enough of that, having to pay for a new Cadillac every year, until the time of Mercedes and a second membership at a better Club? With age, the Devilment's grimace went deep. She got worse, mentally and, not to put a point on it but, she grew disproportionately large in the gluteus maximus. Eyes orbiting, seeking a target, she tongue-thrusted to snatch the unwary, asking point blank for credentials, assets, liabilities and prospects. She needed data for filing. If she felt short shrift, she'd repeat the questions, her pancake layer moving over the sandworms just under the surface. The Devilment and Flossie's son were a match.

She came on strong, teeth, hands and eyes, sucking light like a black hole, as it were. She'd insisted that Mother call her lawyer Sly to handle the situation in Daytona Beach.

Sly advised Mother to leave the kid there, as a lesson.

Mother declined and bailed me out, as the Devilment frothed that a punk could squander his mother's savings and the work Flossie's son had done to earn that money.

The Devilment suffered on that one, and Mother's job came to an end. Cheap clothing was so competitive with so many imposters keeping Flossie's son from his rightful fortune.

Mother could stay, but without pay. Flossie's son and the Devilment delivered the ultimatum on a united front and waited Mother's answer, in case she wanted to stay without pay. Not to worry, he said; he'd make sure she had something to eat. The Devilment grinned in affirmation of something to eat.

Mother became a secretary at United Hebrew Temple, wading into a swift stream where piranha fed on personal stuff, like poverty, divorce, worthless children, a wonderful brother and a sister-in-law too good to be true. The Devilment had set it up. Mother went for a paycheck. These were not country Jews.

She worked, paid the rent and bought groceries. We worked, too, after school and evenings for a print shop, a catering company, a valet parking crew. Brother managed a pizza place. Sissy worked the ambulatory care desk at Jewish Hospital.

Mother quit the temple in a year and got on as an office secretary, until Flossie's son quit the rag business to open a franchise employment agency. The old lament rose again on so many people to support, and he needed help, cheap, front-room defense against bums looking for handouts. And he'd pay, not so much, because Mother would be "a part of the organization."

Warnings from her children went unheard.

The Devilment worked in back, interviewing applicants, asking what they had and who they knew, showing her teeth.

We endured, far from Southern Indiana on a tortuous road to tedium and a suburban high school full of kids who knew everything but didn't know anything.

Mother took us to see her workplace, after hours to avoid conflict. Her desk sat out front. Three more desks each had a private office. Flossie's son had one. The Devilment had the second. The third was for Biffa, introducing the prodigy to success in business.

Biffa drove a new Camaro, because his kind of potential couldn't want for basic transportation. Biffa aspired to be a sports announcer but looked down and mumbled. Short of network stardom, he would be a CPA, or he could inherit the wind.

The office bathroom had a radio. That seemed odd. Mother said Biffa couldn't make tinkle, much less poopy doo-doo, if he thought anyone could hear. The strange cousins had lost their simple color. We laughed short. A simpleton drove a new car to his private office for continued failure in potty training and spoon feedings.

Mother arrived in the old Rambler.

Harsh little truths ornamented our world. Hanging out at an ice cream parlor near the apartment was a far cry from heading up the back steps of The Java Shop at The Hotel Vendome, up to the bookie joint, when I was six and Brother seven.

The bookies and bettors stopped still as a flock, sensing predators and fleeing out windows, across the roof and down the fire escape. Brother and I wanted to play, too, but the old man said, "Stand still for chrissake."

Cops didn't bother guys with kids back then, and it worked, another example of what the old man called good luck. The scramble out the window, across the roof and down the fire-escape was tough to miss, but we were glad to help out.

The St. Louis years were drab and long, working for rent and groceries. Mother felt relief in Sissy's marriage but not so much in her own two more marriages, to guys who couldn't get it any better than the old man could.

Then came the unhappiest time, taking care of her mother, the Flossie one.

Mother's refrain of rolling stones and no moss came back to haunt when I asked, "And just where is your illustrious career headed?"

III

GRIST FOR THE MILL

At sixty-nine, done with secretary jobs and three marriages, Mother began her next indenture: live-in nurse, attendant, cook and maid for Flossie.

Born in 1918, she grew up a second-rate child for about twenty years; female and dimwit were deemed redundant in those days, not in all quarters but most certainly in hers. Of less importance than a male sibling, she was better suited to cleaning and cooking, as he carried the torch for glory.

She'd ignored the old man's opinion, along with Brother's, Sissy's and mine for another twenty years and another thirty. A shot to the heart woke her up but left her groggy.

Flossie saw herself as dowager queen. Mother, Sissy, Brother and I were court attendants. Flossie wanted reverence and sacrifice, as due.

But we were our father's kids, and it didn't play well, what with one thing and another.

Flossie was as flinty as her son, who walked the earth in her image. The strange cousins fit the pattern with dimmer wits, more suitable to Flossie's needs. Revelation came one day, home alone, when Mother copped a look at the will. She, Sissy, Brother and I got nada. After years of servitude, she seemed surprised.

Flossie's son was named executor of Flossie's estate. As the Devilment's best friend, lawyer Sly Albertson had written Flossie's will. The Devilment could not be inner sanctum, but she worked the principals.

Mother named her the Devilment for her gossip, ill will and bugeyes, as if pressured from within and, at last, gaining a foothold in sanctum sanctorum.

We expected nada from Flossie at all times. We wouldn't kowtow. We rejected the dictates of Flossie, her son and the Devilment, even as Mother insisted on our best interests, even as Mother had no interest.

The Holy Grail for years was the Property. Mother's father died in '35, leaving it to Flossie, who remarried at sixty, knowing in her singular way that her second husband's children would try to get what was hers. In another defense against a wicked world, she quitclaimed the Property to her own children. She could have named specific bequeathals, but her son managed the Property and was also executor of her estate. What could go wrong? Quitclaiming the Property in defense against Flossie's second husband's children made sense. The move may have originated with the Devilment and her lawyer, Sly Albertson, and Flossie's son went along. Why not? In the emotional melee, Flossie slipped up, failing to exclude Sissy, Brother and me after years of no contact. Out of sight, out of mind.

The quitclaim got recorded directly, before the Devilment, her lawyer or Flossie's son realized the Property quitclaim included Mother, thereby putting her children into the line of bequeathal. This lapse occurred about the time the Devilment's rear bumper passed XXL, like Pinocchio's nose for lying and, in this case, factoring greed as well.

The quitclaim oversight was a blunder. Flossie's son saw it in '86, in a blaze of light. He called the principals to meet. Lawyer Sly, the Devilment, Flossie and her son convened at Flossie's condo. Mother was invited, too, naturally; she lived there and could prepare something nice. Flossie's son liked chicken salad with mayonnaise, not mustard. And his tea should be scalding hot, to remind him of the world.

These details came from Mother. After preparing, serving, clearing and overhearing, she got called in to sign a second quitclaim deed, a formality, to be sure. "Come on, come on, come on, Sister. We don't have all night!"

This new quitclaim was exactly like the old quitclaim and only needed resigning for rerecording to make it right, because the old one wasn't right and got sent back. The Property could be in jeopardy. It was only a technicality, another like the other.

But Mother had a lapse of her own—a lapse in complaisance and acceptance. What's that smell? Was something burning? Had instincts finally found traction? Or was it simply sulfur? Had Flossie's son or the Devilment uttered ill will on Mother's children? Had they let slip on their wicked solution? Had they bragged on their children's genius and prosperity? Or did Mother see, hear and feel the jive and know the old document was fine?

She said, "No."

The in-law people were gentle at first, patient with her confusion, soothing her with explanation, telling her how things worked, calming the limited one. Mother was sixty-nine and suddenly sick o' their shit. On another "No," she achieved the soothing objective. Those four who cared most for her own best interests dug in, cackling incantation, swooning in God-tongues, lamenting the bastards, spewing statutes.

Mother smelled motive in the Devilment, lawyer Sly, Flossie and her son. It stank. She sensed the problem with the old quitclaim deed from '80; it included her, Sissy, Brother and me. How could we be in line for the Property with no contact, much less no reverence? The in-law people love, love, loved Mother as only flesh and blood can, and it made no sense for Mother to suffer such liability and total loss at the hands of her wicked children, who, let's face it, were no good.

Lo, into the night they wailed and moaned to the witching hour. She who tires first loses. Mother said no again.

It didn't sit well, after all they'd done for her, that she'd try to cheat them like this. They told her she was bad. They beseeched the retarded sister to be happy doing floors so others might protect her from the evil waiting to pounce.

Mother and Cinderella were painfully similar. Both suffered family oppression in secret, fearing hostility, preserving the peace. She refused to sign, thinking that would be that.

Migrations, chance and a sailboat at last had taken me to Hawaii. I spoke with Mother Saturdays, and though careful, she sometimes slipped on a complaint or subtle need for help. If I asked, she said, "Nothing. It's nothing."

Mother worried that Flossie's son would cheat her, but she feared telling me, embarrassed, perhaps, since I'd forewarned and she'd had none of it. Mother kept the new quitclaim effort under wraps. Why worry? She hadn't signed, and bringing it up would only cause more trouble.

Once a week, Flossie's son visited to lament the world, its bastards and the Devilment. They had her number: outside the blood, one more conniver, out to get what wasn't hers and never could be. Flossie and son had known that score since the Devilment tricked him into marriage, looking for a free ride all along. Flossie flogged him with it, so he could see for his own good. Sure, the Devilment let him stick it in there twice that can be proved. She was no good!

Mother's role in these covens was six-course lunch prep for Flossie and son: salad, soup, little sandwiches with no crust, chopped liver on crackers, fruit and cheese and dessert. She left, so they could talk assets in private.

Mother wised up at glacial speed. At some point after she refused the new quitclaim, Flossie's son came unglued. Mother had also refused to administer Flossie's enema, after failing to cut the crust from his sandwich. She hadn't cleaned Flossie's condo to his standards, proving her ultimate failure to appreciate all he'd done for her.

Flossie was out visiting cronies when he came in yelling at Mother for her failures, and he pushed her: once, twice, three times, knocking her down. Mother was seventy.

WWtOMD? What Would the Old Man Do? To within an inch of his life would have begun the response, blood and gore a few yards past the finish line would have wrapped things up. The old man never hit a woman, even Mother, who pressed more buttons than a person should.

I would have flown in to deliver the legacy punch but didn't hear of the crime until two years after the fact. Wanting to keep the peace, Mother said, "He's still my brother." The following week, she prepped lunch for Flossie and son.

In the world of conniving bastards, sneaky Samaritans, average pedestrians and teeming refuse yearning to be free, I did okay. The road went up, down and around, in and out and down and down . . . and up, up, up. I learned of freedom to fail and the grit to go again, as people do. The legacy was in knockdowns as part of the game. Getting up, dusting off and going back in a bit smarter is a cycle that turns down-in-the-dirt to seasoning.

Wandering ceased twenty-two years after Hoosierville Exodus. Roots took hold at last in a Promised Land far away, a place that felt like home. Twenty-two years and many places made Mr. Boll Weevil look stable. I settled in, relaxed and looked back to a situation on hold.

Research was brief. Flossie's Son had managed the Property forever, but since the quitclaim, he'd kept Mother's half of the rent. I called a lawyer and asked for a knockout.

"What do you mean, a knockout?"

"Just that. I want to take him out. Don't you watch? Get him on the ropes. Hit him in the kidneys. Uppercut, box his ears, wallop his head, kick his ribs, you know, these are the championship rounds?"

"I get it. We have personal animosity."

"We do. Can you take this?"

"Let me see what I can do."

"Fine," I said. "Can you call me next week?"

At first provocation—legal murmurs—Flossie's son put the Property up for sale, a questionable effort to minimize liability, I thought. I was wrong. It was another attempted theft.

Mother didn't know it was for sale. The new lawyer told her. Flossie's son assured her, "Oh, yes! It's time!"

Time took a while, but when a good offer finally came, she needed to sign, a mere formality on escrow instructions. Mother thought that sounded reasonable, time to let bygones go among family, after all. But she put on her reading glasses, to the dismay and chagrin of her own flesh and blood.

The aftershock lingered, as she asked over and again, "My own brother! Did you ever?"

Mother knew nothing of instructions to escrow or much of anything outside a kitchen or department store. But her instincts got sharp on her status in that clan: handmaid, special sister with bad children, to be handled accordingly. She read slowly, pointing with a finger. Escrow was instructed to disburse all proceeds, about a half million, to Flossie's son.

He swore it was an oversight. He would have shared. He would have cared for her as always.

Flossie wailed, "Your own flesh and blood!" She weaved and bobbed, nearly falling. "Your own flesh and blood!" Hinting a fall was meant to cleave the heavens on God's wrath. Look out! She sobbed, squeezing her fingers, money seeping from her grasp, her good works, thoughts and prayers coming to naught. She wept. She whined, "Your own flesh and blood!" She went to tongues on the direct hotline—a mix of Hebrew prayers and gibberish. God would make things right. She got up for a wobble but sat down and wailed.

Mother saw, as if for the first time, the dog and pony before her, its trickery and deceit more disappointing than the wrong man in marriage. She'd been born into the wrong family, a stunning revelation. How could . . . She worked it, untangling the knots, asking the thin air, "My own brother?"

We'd grown accustomed, if not tolerant, to Mother and the in-law shitshow. We didn't bear down or one-up; didn't say we'd told her so. She'd suffered the curse by birth. Luckily, as the freak of that nature, she came to see the truth. We'd advised of the curse for years; her kith and kin were foul, but we needed to press no further. Mother became her grandest inquisitor.

The Property was set to close, ending the whole sick affair. "Isn't that best? Can't we let the *tsouris* go?" Flossie pleaded, as if "letting the trouble go" would expunge her guilt.

"Yes, we can. But no," Mother said.

"What do you mean, no? Haven't you and your children bled him dry? Hadn't you taken what was naturally his?"

Mother and her children wanted the affair over, and over it would be, on a fair divvy of the moolah la. That would be an equal disbursement from escrow on the sale, and return of the stolen rent money.

"Wha!"

No need to belabor Flossie's fit. She went in short order from *schpielkies* (very upset) to *verklempt* (suffering tremors) to *fablunged* (half crazy) to *meshuga* (all crazy).

We didn't call it the fun part but tasted sweetness. The stolen rent would have resolved Mother's poverty in those years of theft, would have brought her up from hand-to-mouth scrimp and scrabble. It would have covered basics, rent and groceries for those years, seven of them, or, in monthly units, ninety-six of them. As half owner of the commercially zoned Property, she'd gotten nada, zip, bupkis.

The core foundation of Mother's interest was that she'd loved her father, and he'd loved her in return. Whether that love was actual or presumed, we can only speculate. He checked out early, about age forty-one, of leukemia. I sense the love was actual because Mother reflected it. Moreover, the bequeathal to Mother was legal, as if karmic.

But Flossie's son had taken it all. We could also speculate on where it went. The Mercedes (leased)? The Devilment's dream membership in two clubs instead of one? Biffa's new Camaro (leased)? Dreba's hopes and aspirations? Long past presidential, she sustained dire need of wardrobe and many specialists.

Half the rent on the Property came to a hunk o' dough from '83 to '92. Repayment would require a cash outlay for Flossie's son. He must have paid tax on rental income, but could he claim repayment of stolen funds as a business deduction? Well, lawyer

Sly, ace accountant Biffa and Flossie's son could surely figure that out.

We tasted more sweetness. The trial would be another show, Executive Producer: God. Associate Producer: the old man. Director: me.

I savored prospects beyond legal and financial; such a social-climbing bunch would squirm over truths made public. Could we pursue a felony indictment? I thought we could. I looked into it, feeling no emotion, a conspicuous absence to be proud of, though I was excited for Mother. She'd see me in a memorable suit, in court at last, for the prosecution.

Players and facts would become accountable, prima facie. Volition and justice came around like stellar bodies, completing their orbits. We would rise and fall, sing out and wail, at last revealing the people we had become or were all along.

Mother eclipsed her former self, stepping forth at seventy-three. Small fits had relieved the pressure of the in-laws ganging up to keep her down. She'd blown her stack when we made jokes about Flossie or her son, but she stopped. Brother's stand-up of Flossie threatening to die was a ringer, but she wouldn't laugh.

She molted, stood taller, and we proceeded to litigation, no more Gothic Cinderella but a phenomenon to behold, geriatric Wonder Woman on a mission. Then again, newfound fortitude was intermittent. She knew but denied. She wished they hadn't. She still made sandwich quarters when Flossie's son came for "business" with Flossie.

"Why?"

"They have to eat," she said.

Between the sale of the Property and the trial, another truth emerged: a lifetime of faith had been misplaced. Knowing and denying affected her speech, taking her down to phrases. Depressed and dazed, she stared off.

She learned by statute and section that her children's indictment of the in-laws was accurate. Flossie's son had lied and stolen on grins and bad intentions.

"After all these years," Mother said, over and over. "Devotion . . . Duty . . . Love . . ." She muttered frequently, often taking a seat to mutter more. She was down.

Litigation turned on the lights in Flossie's kitchen, where her son scurried, caught out.

"What are you trying to do?" He wailed. "You just want your children to get this money, don't you?"

"Don't you?" Mother asked back.

IV

ROMANCE GOES AWAY

Nearly thirty years after the old man checked out, he lingered. Lasting love came up for review, when I returned to St. Louis for the trial. We kept Mother distracted, turning to positive topics or facsimiles thereof, so she could look up, not down. Old stories came up for embellishment, including the one of the second proposal.

Did the old man ever love her?

"Stupid question," I said. "Does anybody ever love anyone? Or did they? Or could they? It comes and goes. So what?"

Hearing her fickle son, she shook her head. She'd loved and been loved, but not so much in marriage. Had she loved him? No, not since he swept her away on fun and affluence but defaulted to no milk for her children. Elaborating yet again on distress from way back, she could forget the toxic stew simmering on the front burner. So we looked into old love, its ups and downs.

"He was a player and got lucky but went cold," I said. "It happens, sooner or later. You drove him nuts and left. I think it was more practical than heartfelt."

"I felt it," she said. "You're so smart. He wanted me back."

Wha? Who knew?

They met by chance on a street downtown halfway through the year that began with divorce and ended in death. He saw her, stepped up and dropped to a knee like he had in '41, when the world shone. The second time was somber; he said nothing would change, could he come home? It got to her; she couldn't say no but couldn't say yes. She walked away.

The end.

She looked down to where she'd arrived: end of story, past and present seemed equally devoid.

Her children saw, emotion plummeting, going gray. So we picked up the old review, seeking something, somewhere, somehow, that might soften the old, hard-boiled assessments.

He was a building contractor after oil, before diamonds. I was three, or six. In those days of split-level ranch-style, the '50s, our life shrank into a smaller house each year, from grand construction to low rent. Domestic pressure rose on cross purpose and no joy. Proposal and rejection on the street in '61 came as natural as grit on pavement.

"Natural for you," Sissy said. "Bold for him."

"He was good at that," Mother said, scorning the game spirit and zest for good times.

"Why do you resent that? It's the best legacy we have. It's in the clan, and that's us," Brother said.

"Call it what you want," she said. "I know what I know."

Assessments would not change, no surprise. But we'd anesthetized a morning, looking at the past instead of the moment upon us. What's the difference between benevolent and malevolent? We felt justice on the way; she felt sadness and shame. Oddly, it seemed like a fine line, and to shore up distraction for that session, I posed the tough question: "Don't we have your best interests in mind?"

She got it, nodding at last at the tough truth her children had revealed.

Brother took the baton and stayed out front on reflections, with doubts in hot pursuit. He told of Flossie's Saturday pattern, waiting till Mother had gone to Brother's place for a few hours of relief and solace. In that interim, Flossie would have her weekly seizure and call Mother to say goodbye. Mother was meant to rush back to plead no, not today! Please!

On recent Saturdays, Flossie had quacked until the paramedics took her to the hospital with her full-time attendant, Mother, who'd rushed back, as beckoned. Flossie hated stretchers and wanted a sedan chair with four fellows to carry instead of two. She wanted to sit up, to see and better manage the situation.

Brother said the Saturday pattern had become a script, an old one, enjoying a very long run because of Flossie's insistence on dying and Mother's weakness in responding, until Mother's best failure yet. Fatigue can grant insight; she stopped running home, stopped begging Flossie not to die.

Flossie had taken to calling back to whisper something selfless, as if from the other side. "Where is the silver polish?"

She didn't want to polish the silver. She wanted "the new girl" to do it. The new girl was not a nurse. Who needs a nurse for what they charge? Steal your money is what they do. A "girl" was cheap and not so hoity-toity. Who ever heard of paying somebody by the hour to sit there? And who paid for the air-conditioning while the girl sat there? Did you ever?

The girl had no name because of heavy turnover. The girl that day was sixty and quit the following week.

Mother laughed, even as the stories took another toll.

Flossie was ninety-four, mobile and alert, ready to produce the show as necessary and, lo and behold, the phone rang. It was Flossie, calling Mother to say she felt bad, but don't worry that she might die; yes, perhaps, on that very day.

Mother said, "Aw, shit," like the old man when a duck dove on his bait. Was she supposed to end a rare visit with her children for this drill? The short answer was no. Nobody asked who would care if Flossie croaked.

Sitting speechless, phone in hand, Mother seemed clear on not going but conflicted on the question. What if?

Meanwhile, Flossie had handed the phone to the new girl, who said, "Yes, Ma'm. She lay her own self down on the carpet and give me the number. She want a ambulance. They on the way."

Weak all over one more time, Mother asked if Brother would drive her to the hospital.

Brother perked, not only willing but enjoying the show. With me along, it could only get better.

I declined, until Brother promised an outing to remember and a joint on the way.

"Oh no," Mother said. "You're not smoking that stuff with me in the car. I'll be sick."

"Go get in the car," Brother said. "We'll smoke it in here."

"We've got to hurry!" Mother said.

"For what?" Brother said. "She'll be dead a long time."

Sissy took her leave.

We arrived at the hospital just before the ambulance, and in came Flossie on the stretcher with the girl in tow. She wailed when she saw us and waved Mother over.

I hadn't seen Flossie in twenty years.

She blinked and yelled for the doctor, "Right now! I'm ready to die!" Clutching her jaw, she shrieked, "The cheese! Get the cheese! It's killing me! The cheese!" The cyst on her jaw filled with smegma. No matter how badly it needed squeezing, the thoughtless bastards couldn't get it right. The new girl wouldn't squeeze it, and with so much money spent to be there (Medicare) the least these bastards could do was squeeze the cheese.

The plot thickened when Flossie's son arrived, just after sedation. Striding forth, he accused Mother of negligence, calling Brother a bum and taking command.

I stepped up.

He stopped, sensing where we'd left off.

Mother had learned a new posture by then, beyond the putty heretofore. We hadn't seen the measure of her resolve until she, too, stepped up to protect her children or dare another shove. She told him to shut up.

He did, stuttering that she didn't have to be so mean.

Brother stepped up, too, for the tag team challenge, but Flossie's son turned away, old and confused and way too shrunken to tangle.

The Devilment in this wake debriefed the doctors, grinning in acute concern for the fragile life about to trigger her inheritance. Where did they live? Were they Jewish? Which club? Did they know the joy of Mercedes? She made it plain to see: she was different, like them.

It came to naught. Sedation and sleep. Game over.

On the way home, Brother said, "The cheese! It's killing me." We finished our joint as Mother reflected on the cheese, opening up, offloading in her way, ditching another burden.

Brother asked, "You squeezed the cheese?"

She said he talked like a fool and laughed, and we knew: she'd squeezed the cheese.

Our rolling confessional loosened more, secondhand smoke easing the bindings. She said squeezing the cheese was nothing compared to the enema. It was the enema that did her in.

Flossie had wanted Mother to give the enema for years, but Mother said no, she would not give the enema. Flossie told her to ask a neighbor, and Mother knocked on doors down the hall. "Will you give the enema?"

All refused, some politely.

Flossie had wailed like an old Jew at the wall. Please, after a lifetime of devotion, will somebody give the enema?

Mother finally put a foot down. "I told her; I won't give the enema. And I won't. She can call her son to give the enema."

"That's right," Brother said. "Let him give the enema."

"You know what she did?" Mother asked.

"No," I said. "What did she do?"

Flossie had wailed, "You *could* give the enema!" She wailed on; let the neighbors hear, so they could know that Mother refused, that Mother was a bad daughter.

"The neighbors bolted their doors, didn't they?" I asked. "If you wouldn't give the enema, they knew you'd be back. Because one of them *could* give the enema. Right? Am I right?"

"What a fool I've been," Mother said.

"Yes," I said, "You keep saying that, then you follow up with more foolishness."

"Not this time," Mother said. "I can't give the enema. Even if I wanted to, I couldn't."

"But you don't want to, do you?" Brother asked.

Mother said her position was not rational but heartfelt. She had made it clear that she would not give the enema. She could not give the enema.

Flossie was beside herself, so stuffed with baked chicken and matzo balls, gefilte fish and little sandwiches with the crust trimmed off. She'd had no enema since the last girl gave her one and quit, good for nothing. "And she was Catholic, too," Flossie had said. "They usually hang on for a while."

Problems continued to back up, clogging the drains.

Mother didn't need to say it again: no, she would not give the enema. Nor would she remind Brother what a boorish troublemaker he could be.

Robert Wintner

"At least the trial ought to clear things out. Don't you think? A legal Roto-Rooter, you know, clearing the shit so the money can flow. Something like that."

Mother looked out the window to ask the cloudy gray sky, "Why would he want to do that?"

"Why would he do what?" Brother asked.

"You know, try to get me to sign a new paper."

"Which paper?" Brother asked. "You mean the new quitclaim to take the Property from you? Or do you mean instructions to escrow to give him all the money?"

"I don't know," Mother said, slipping again. "I don't know why he would do that."

"Why he would do what?" Brother asked. Mother needed repetition, to let the truth sink in.

Brother and I took her back to Flossie's place, so she could prepare more soup, baked chicken, snacks and sandwiches for Flossie's return from the hospital. She'd called herself a fool and stayed a fool. But on that day of change, she gained character and intention. Still stuck in old habits, she felt the bad blood picking up like a current.

She told us to come up. In the gloomy, mothball air of Flossie's condo, Mother went to Flossie's will, having searched and found it in recent days. She told us what Flossie had promised her and then read the will aloud. It left a half mil or so to Flossie's son and then to his children Dreba and Biffa. It left Mother's children five hundred bucks. It left Mother nothing.

She'd known it, but reading it aloud was her epiphany, ugly, painful and too long avoided. She'd grown up on a cast-iron rule

132

to mistrust the world and its people, so many immoral, mean and unrelated sonsabitches. Blood ties were to lie down and die for, and she would have, pushing her children as well to do the right thing, to call Flossie on her birthday. "Do the right thing. I only want you to do the right thing."

We went home. T minus two days and counting on close of escrow. The trial was five days out.

The next day, she showed Flossie the will and asked, "What is this? What does this mean? How can you do this?"

Flossie was meek, perhaps ready to die again. She whined, "Your own flesh and blood. Your own flesh and blood. He has your best interests at heart. Your best interests. Why wouldn't he take care of you? He's always taken care of you."

Closing on the Property was rote, physical presence not required. We were there to assure smooth movement and Mother's fair share. I counseled silence and restraint for a change, advising Mother not to tell her story of injustice, ingratitude and degradation suffered at the hands of Flossie's son.

But she couldn't hold back, not with lawyers, escrow agents, secretaries and defendants there to hear it. She did okay, focused on the correction at hand and scoring at will.

The Devilment chattered, explaining the radio voice in the bathroom as it got louder. "It's the most unusual thing. He practically runs our company and knows more about accounting than most CPAs. He's a sports announcer, too."

I asked, "He carries a radio?"

Brother went to the bathroom door and knocked. "We can hear you. Biffa. We can hear you."

Flossie's son stood.

I also went to the bathroom door, to knock and advise, "No squeezing, Big Fella."

The escrow officer was ready for signatures. Biffa missed it, stuck on Top 40, trying to relax and give, knowing that people outside could hear and visualize.

Mother signed here and here and here, as the officer instructed, and Brother and I approved.

Near the bottom of the stack, I asked, "How do you feel?"

"I'm fine."

"Can you feel your dirty little mitts on the moolah yet?"

"Almost."

"Do you feel good about that?"

"Yes."

"Good. Now, look at your brother and the Devilment."

"What for?"

"To tell them."

"Tell them what?"

"Tell them to kiss your ass."

Well, that got her laughing through the tension. We all knew a legacy motto when we heard it, and she felt the other current, the good blood that bonded her children. It differed from what she came from. I think she came over to the right side of the family that day, and we took her in.

V

AROUND THE CLUBHOUSE TURN

Escrow closed, and so did contentions on disbursement of proceeds. Blinders off, Mother saw the truth and let up on bittersweet recollection of what she'd called "all those years," meaning her Cinderella years of youth and her Hausfrau years of disappointment.

The Property was a milestone. Old stories, places and events had defined us. New time took shape on a glimpse at the future. Like most transitions, an event would catalyze change. The trial loomed, as poignant as truth and justice can be, pitting the defendant, Flossie's son, against a judge on a charge of theft.

Deposition, discovery, duck, dodge and hide had taken three years. Mother complained: it dragged on so long. Enough.

I told her: justice takes time.

From London and Paris, visiting friends, I'd come to St. Louis a week before the trial. The trial felt like a reckoning. It would culminate the years of waiting. All those years?

Flossie's son squirmed. First, we would dive deep into his pocket for a hundred-thousand dollars, or we would chase him around the block with our figurative frying pan: judgments, collections, liens and garnishments. Second would be the consequence of theft, moving the unfortunate situation from civil court to criminal. Third would be the vindication I longed for, as much in the process as in the catch. It had begun. He and I both feared it. I wanted to pop him in the nose as just response from a kid getting chased by a nasty man with a frying pan. How much would that punch cost? I calculated the long and short of it.

I thought of letting it go. Hadn't Flossie's son paid his debt to the demons he served? Old and shrunk, he capitalized on sympathy with a wobble and a matching smile, as if.

I stopped pondering punches and potentials and let nature take its course. Events would unfold on virtues or lack thereof. The Devilment would quack, but who would listen? Making such noise with an ass as sprawled as a Midwest suburb, she looked and sounded like gridlock at rush hour, Exhibit A for the prosecution.

We convened at the lawyer's office the day before the trial.

Mother whined, "What if he doesn't have the money? He's my brother!"

"He can mortgage the house," I consoled. "He can sell some cars or get a loan. If we get lucky on the criminal side, I'll lend him the money for his new striped suit. Scratch that. I'll pay for it. We are family, after all."

Mother could not fathom Flossie's son in jail. I could. I told her not to worry; the Devilment could explain his new work in South America, as necessary, building bridges.

Our lawyer held back, a disappointment, also thinking criminal prosecution excessive.

I explained, "This is an exercise in law on a theft case. If we prove theft, should he not do time? Isn't that what convicted criminals do?"

The lawyer and Mother shared a tepid scowl. I did not ask if he'd taken a course in law school on ignoring the facts. I let it go, for the time being. "Thirty days in the County Jail would be a tasty chestnut to chew at the Club. Wouldn't it?"

"You're crazy," Mother said.

I didn't feel crazy. A bit eager, maybe, pursuing justice on a crime or crimes in a series. I imagined punching the defendant in the nose, and the judge banging his gavel. "Sustained!" I laughed alone.

I stayed at Brother's house on the fold-out couch. He'd picked me up at the airport after a long, miserable day in the friendly skies, London to St. Louis.

Winging far north, the Arctic permafrost glared to thirty thousand feet, unbroken but for a few Quonset huts or igloos, sparse flecks on the frosting. Bitter cold and blizzard winds brought these folk together in community. Who would live there by choice, and why? Splinters pierced the crust, some with chimneys wisping smoke. Hours across that tundra granted insight to liquor as the key to sanity or the exit.

Were they descended from first people or first migrants, Mongolians or Slavs seeking routes or escape? I imagined their life and wanted to feel it but couldn't, just as I couldn't imagine holding back on Flossie's son. How did anyone live so isolated, bleak and cold, or let go of a grudge? How did anyone get there? Could they get out?

Could they make such warmth among themselves, because they loved the place like home? Did that warmth come from the heart, or was it learned from warm-hearted parents? Did they follow the Ice King's beneficent rule? Did they follow parental blueprint?

Character derives from nature and nurture. Hot and cold, cruelty and compassion, right and wrong form on genetics and training, from DNA and example. Babies look up at birth to bond with creatures nearby. Children learn rules and standards. Could these people have gained a standard of warmth by evolution? I thought they could and must have done so.

I'd read of Tibetan monks living among icy peaks and frozen whispers. Disciples bring water and food to sustain the hermetic life. Do monks in meditation help resolve chaos in the world?

I ordered a brandy for warmth. I'd felt formative for a long time. I'd learned fair play. It seemed straightforward.

Meditation ended on a voice command, time to lower the shades for a slam-dunk competition, *Brady Bunch* reruns, *Night Court* and a bad movie, as if that pablum was a better view.

A few hours later, the shades stayed down, most folks having missed the view when the shades were up.

Thirteen hours from takeoff, St. Louis came on with compression. Brother had his new Bronco and a joint ready for reentry, a tradition to mollify first takes on family aging since the last visit, a year or two ago. We diffused mortality with a joint and eased in with a few jokes.

Sissy's son came for the ride, J. Woodrow, in his second year of college, home for Chanukah. We sat in front, J. Woody in the middle, not moving but staring, until Woody said, "Let's go." Woody thought his uncles fairly nuts. It felt gratifying and confirmed our two-way generation gap.

"We want to talk about your drug problem," Brother said.

"I don't have one," Woody said.

Brother turned. "We know." He lit the joint.

Woody said he didn't smoke the stuff, especially during the week.

We passed it past him, until Brother asked if he understood the potential for bad blood in the family.

Woody nodded, a college kid seeking understanding. He took a few hits to get blasted with his uncles, so the next generation wouldn't feud.

At the parking-lot exit, Brother gave the attendant his ticket and a twenty, as Woody leaned over to ask, "Hey, how do you get a nun pregnant?" The attendant made change as Woody yelled, "You fuck her!"

Brother and I didn't laugh but felt hopeful at prospects for an heir. Pulling out, Woody asked, "Hey, what's the worst thing about being an atheist?" We gave up. "No one to talk to when you're getting head!"

"A college education," Brother said.

"Only the best," I said.

"Fucking right," Woody said. "Four grand a semester." This was a long time ago, 1992, when four grand was big, and an airport pickup meant parking, so family could go in to greet at the gate.

St. Louis in January is as cold as Labrador. The wind howled like lost souls. Little gusts felt like death in flurries, and St. Louis flickered in a darker shade of gray. Anticrime lights in bilious amber discouraged muggers crazy enough to be out. Also softly glowing, thousands of TVs and other lights in buildings where people would work or shop tomorrow and forever.

What was new? Brother said he'd worried for a long time that Mother would die before Flossie. He'd come to think he might die before Flossie. His suburb looked like Smallville, the little town built for Lionel Electric Trains, laid out on plywood, with a train station and a lantern guy going in and out, in and out. Big action on Main Street was the Hobby Shop, selling little cars, boats and airplanes that really ran.

Thoughts like these are best left unsaid. Stoned to the gills, not speaking is easy, possibly natural.

And stoned to the gills allowed forgetfulness, too. I forgot that Brother's new Bronco was a foot higher off the ground than a car, so I opened the door to step out on Brother's driveway but fell out, into the dirty snow, its icy stink rising like cold ammonia. Brother and Woody laughed, as Mother stuck her head out to ask what was wrong.

I called, "My slip forked!" I got up to avoid further ridicule. "What a great town. It's got everything."

Brother yelled to get my goddamn suitcase so he could pull into the garage.

Mother called to hurry in, sit and eat, while it's hot.

Inside, Woody wanted to share his adventure, hands out, as if to fly. He giggled and talked stupid. "Geez, those colors."

Brother and I laughed. Mother didn't get it, so Woody lit the roach and inhaled big, as seen in movies.

Mother still didn't get it, serving perfectly browned potatoes, overboiled broccoli, baked chicken and carrots, her specialty, with squashes, greens, more potatoes, twice-baked, and vegetable barley soup, an old fave. She served quick, anxious that we'd been there three minutes and had yet to eat, with cookies, cakes and ice cream on deck.

Woody passed the roach. Brother took a hit and passed it to me with the broccoli.

Mother got it: "Oh, my God! You're smoking that LSD. I'm going to be sick."

Woody got another lesson in family play when Brother said, "I'm going to be sick, too. I don't know why he brings this stuff to town. Is this why we send him to college?"

Woody looked for help but too late. "Me, too," I said. "Four grand a semester, and for what? So he can come home like a drug addict and drag us down with him. This stuff is poison!"

Woody cried foul.

Mother said, "Put that away and eat! Now!" She served and watched, watched and served. And homecoming was official.

I woke the next morning at first light on a phone call from Mother. She'd driven back to Flossie's after dinner and would be over again in an hour or two but knew I'd be up from jet lag. She needed to know what I wanted for breakfast. She reviewed Brother's fridge, shelf by shelf, so jam-packed the door wouldn't seal. A chair tilted back on two legs, the top of it under the fridge handle, kept it shut.

I assured her I'd find something to eat.

She called back to remind me of bagels, eggs, coffee cake, pastries and, of course, what was left of dinner.

"Why are you up?" I asked.

"I get up at five. I like to get an early start."

"Good thing you called," I said. "I'm starving and can't find anything to eat."

Catching on yet again, she said, "Wait till you're a mother."

I had coffee, amazed at Brother's kitchen. Mid-forties already, his kitchen connected to the past, shoring up for hard times, prepped for another Great Depression.

"I'm from the Depression," Mother often explained, headed to a crosstown market for toothpaste on sale. She'd pick up a year's supply for Brother and me. She mailed mine, a tube or two at a time with a note: *Do you need toothpaste?* and a reminder, *You must shop the sales!*

I had explained the false value of toothpaste futures.

She listened with pity, like I knew nothing from nothing, and a Depression would open my eyes.

While nailing the toothpaste deal crosstown, she'd pick up a five-pound bag of sugar; what the hell. But the bastards got her for a buck eighty-five, and she found the same bag the next day for a buck fifteen. So, it was back across, Brother or I protesting the miles, the time, the gas, the wear and tear to save a few cents.

Protests were weak next to Mother's compulsion. "What? You think I'm nuts? Besides, we have to go anyway."

We had to go anyway for onions at twenty-seven cents a pound less than on our side of town, and if you don't think it adds up on a twenty-pound bag, well, she had news for you. Grocery trips often included return items, items purchased in faith that pricing could go no lower, yet the price plummeted in the next day or two, sometimes to a dollar less. Brother got used to it or at least expected it. I never did. When a store manager asked what was wrong, and Mother told them the price was sixty cents less across town, I explained again, "She's from the Depression. The Great Depression. She's from it." Store managers accepted, to get on with their lives.

Brother's kitchen was small, four strides across when empty, back when Earth first cooled and eons of sedimentation hadn't yet layered to form a crust. By late Twentieth century, a man could pivot slowly, seeking a foothold and balance, fridge to stove.

The pantry held twelve cases of Acme Cola in a mix: Diet Acme, Classic Acme, New Acme and Caffeine Free Acme in both Diet Classic and Diet New. Acme Cola came in cans or bottles and looked like Coca Cola but cost less. Buying Acme was small rebellion. As Brother put it, "Why pay more?" The gross national product seemed literal, counting dollars spent on sugar water with bubbles.

Rounding out the pantry: a case of olives, two gallons of pickled okra, canned goods for a crew of nine adrift for a week and two bags of dog biscuits, twenty-five pounds each. Outside the pantry: foothills of bags, paper and plastic, tinfoil, rubber bands, empty jars and boxes and many balls of string that unraveled in odd lengths, two inches to two feet, though most of the two-footers were spliced shorties. Mother often said, "It's good to have some long string ready to go."

A Sarah Lee Pound Cake foil box a few years old sat on the stacks of empty containers, used and washed many times, soft like old denim. It held eggs wrapped in Kleenex.

Why?

Brother said Mother put them there, he didn't know why.

I asked Mother.

She grimaced, like I'd asked which child should live, and said, "You talk so crazy."

Beside the eggs in tissue: wads of plastic bags in plastic bags. Rubber bands in jars and plastic bags in jars and jars in cabinets that could not close on so many jars. Brother's two old toasters lay buried on the counter under a Busch Bavarian clock, dusty and dead at four thirty. More bags, boxes and tubs of forks, plastic and metal, odd spoons and knives and two sets of GINSU knives, as seen on TV, an amazing value at not $49.95, not $39.95, no, not even $29.95, but yours today for only $19.95, guaranteed sharp for fifty years. And if you order today, you get the slicer, the dicer, the peeler and this amazing paring knife worth $60 all by itself!

Brother had two sets in case, you know . . . And fifty years rolls around before you know it. The second set waited under a small mountain of pens and pencils, some collectible, showing presidential candidates of the '60s.

Folded rags covered most flat places, among active rags hanging from faucets and cabinet handles. Brother had the G.E. iron Mother got in '37, as a girl. She used it through her lives, marriages and moves, until Brother got his own house in '81, or '86 and needed an iron, a good one.

She'd demonstrated, wadding the shirts and grabbing water from the faucet into the shirt for ironing. Not too quick but waiting for even absorption.

A banged-up Mr. Coffee slumped front and center. A new Mr. Coffee, still in the box, on sale, sat under the sink with more rags, bags and jars. The new unit had waited since '72 for the old one to stop working.

I got my first boat job in '72, on a shrimp trawler out of Ocracoke, North Carolina. A WW I vintage PT boat, *Edith* went sixty-five feet, last of the splinter fleet, all wood, stem to stern, built late in the campaign, 1918, the year Mother was born. Jeffrey Baxter owned *Edith* and saw me coming down the dock, a lubberly kid from Hoosierville. He also heard the lie, that I'd worked boats before. A kid with sea time would have shut up, would have shown what he'd seen in his eyes.

But Jeffrey'd slung some bullshit in his time, too, and needed crew and said, "Four-thirty tomorrow morning." I showed up in the dark and imagined *Edith* slicing into dawn. Built like

Ma Kettle, she looked tough and indifferent, massive at the dock, and she stayed big in the channel, heading out to the sound.

She shrank to proportion in open water. Sunrise broke yellow gray over bilious swells from two directions. In my face: salt spray, diesel fumes and ocean glory at long last by five thirty. Sick by six, breakfast time, I looked up to see Jeffrey come from his tiny galley with a paper plate of boiled shrimp.

"Lucky you," I said, like he couldn't see the green in my gills. "Get to eat shrimp every day! Boy."

Jeffrey spoke the Cockney dialect of the Hoi Toiders who immigrated from London, East End, to North Carolina, Outer Banks, to fish and spawn. "Thar's a hoi toid on a sewth soid."

He scoffed, "Maggits. At's all ey is. Maggits." He ate two at once with disgust, the legs dangling from his lips while he chewed. Jeffrey thought peeling shrimp was wasting time. He ate them whole, heads on. "Em's a juiciest parts!" He thought deveining another waste. "Srimp veins is shit," and it was high time—hoi toim—them people knew it didn't make no difference, "gittin' a dukey out, if they's eatin' maggits." He shoveled two more into the hopper, crushing on one side, sorting shmush with his tongue, dribbling shell fragments and nasty debris out the other side. Chewed bits tumbled onto his chest, and he laughed again at the sheer notion of luck on guys like him or me.

He didn't even look when I lunged another heave over the rail. He knew. "You moit git owver it. You moit not. Aw roit, let's get 'em in." He meant the nets. He dropped the winches into gear, casual as a corporate man slips into a suit coat. He let the catch bags over, then the nets and tickle chains.

I watched like spore growth, until Jeffrey realized too late the hazards of a lubber on a work boat. Witless, I watched the tickle chain uncoil to slide across the deck and wrap my ankle on the way over the rail. Spinning in air, I grabbed the rail with both hands and hung on.

Jeffrey jumped to the steel-lipped oak doors and heaved them forward to gain a few seconds before they'd drop in, as designed, yanking me to ninety feet with the half-ton rig.

Jumping to where I hung on, he jammed his fingers under my wrists and said, "Twarl yer lags! Gentle like! Slow down! Relax . . . Now!" I did, and the chain let go a blink before the big doors tipped off, swung out and splashed to a mess o' bubbles with little last gasps inside. Or maybe that was me. He pulled me aboard. He said, "Stand over yonder" and worked it alone.

At the end of the day, he didn't fire me but said he couldn't pay me on days I didn't work. I stayed on, fairly worthless. It wasn't a question of proving anything to myself or Jeffrey or making money. I'd given up the proving bullshit years before, at nine or eleven, when Mother kept saying what I'd proved every time I took the bit in my teeth and slogged to victory. I'd told her eighty cents an hour was shit, not proof. I realized by ten or twelve that Mother was confused as well on what builds character. A smart man knows when to cut his losses. Or a boy.

The money wasn't in shrimping anyway. Oh, it was big dough the year before, when a crew percentage could go to hundreds of dollars a week. But the year I went, every trawler from the Outerbanks to the Sea Islands focused on Port Royal and Calibogue Sounds. No, it wasn't the money.

I stayed on for the dream nurtured since *The Seventh Voyage of Sinbad*. I needed to go. I sure as hell didn't want a career on a shrimp boat, not after what I'd seen, but how could I handle the open sea and a world of adventure, puking on six-foot swells that weren't even breaking?

Sue picked me up that first afternoon and every afternoon.

Jeffrey stared, impolitely, longing to show her the rule of the sea. He seemed harmless, a young man at sea. He said a few weeks in that his wife had died that year. He was thirty-one. "She'uz twenty-eight and purty as a picture. I swar it. Purty as yer wife. We had us two kids. They's still up home." Jeffrey didn't cry but two tears rolled, as if his story had happened like breakfast had happened, and shrimp drivel and tears accompany those things. We got the nets over with much less fuss.

I never got to a hundred percent on deck work and machinery but probably got to ninety-five. I kept my coffee down, leapt from rail to rail and gobbled maggots with a laugh, heads on, in roly poly waves and diesel dust.

Jeffrey came over for dinner a few times. He wore a white shirt and aftershave and once brought a bushel of crabs and showed us how to prep for the griddle without the guts or boiling the flavor out.

I'd anticipated a life of it but only stayed on a few weeks, scoring more grease, rot, salt, gut pounding, hangover, instant death and maggots than glory or money. We had a few adventures, like engine failure in a heavy ebb, when Jeffrey went below for eight hours on a fast drift to sea at a hundred degrees below deck. He fixed it. I monitored the bilge pumps, running straight off the batteries, and kept a few boys apprised of our status on the radio. We snagged a hulk in a net one day and couldn't back off and faced major loss on the net, the chains and doors—half a season's work. Jeffrey dove on it, thirty-five, forty feet he figured, hand over handing down the drag cable into the murk. He didn't like that stuff but loved not knowing what each day would bring, and I felt his trust, once we learned my capacity and limitations. I valued that most of all.

Life is full of changes, some of them from one thing to the opposite. I came to see bottom trawlers as ocean death machines, destroying benthic habitat and species like no tomorrow. We didn't know that, back in '72, when the world was endless, the oceans limitless. Time with Jeffrey and his trust have lingered.

Those days mostly brought the sea, as anticipated. As yet unimagined was the carnage of nets. Every species living in those waters got dumped dead on deck, called "trash fish" in the industry, failing to convert to dollars. Rays, turtles, sharks, eels, fishes rendered worthless by a world outracing its headlights.

Equally amazing: the try-net, a smaller version of the big nets, brought up every ten minutes on a small winch and emptied on deck, contents extrapolated on shrimp ratio and volume of the catch. Too full, the big nets would not come up or risk breaking heavy hardware. Also in the try, sea life of spectacular wonder.

Who knew? Lowcountry seas stay murky on suspended particulates. I found a few sheets of glass leaning on a barn and cut and glued them into a tank one Sunday and set it up with a filter and pump and filled it with seawater. I kept a bucket on deck for transfer of survivors: blowfish, batfish, butterfish, sea robins, fantail filefish, upside-down filefish, pipefish, and once an Atlantic giant seahorse.

Jeffrey couldn't fathom messing with anything he couldn't eat, keeping them alive for a tank to watch. Forty years down the road, having arrived in the Promised Land, I spent a half million bucks toward ending the aquarium trade in Hawaii and around the world. Change happens, often for the best. Ocean habitat and species seemed durable in '72, and murky water left humanity clueless on the havoc wreaked. Forty years later, a better response was way past due.

We hit bonanzas on big nets full of nothing but shrimp. On one occasion, Jeffrey showed his ocean soul, when the barometer dropped two millibars and the VHF buzzed with hurricane chatter. The fleet went in, leaving Port Royal Sound to us. As Jeffrey put it, we tore 'm up. Those were the last days of endless extraction, too many boats taking ocean wildlife.

We headed in at dusk on ten-foot seas breaking over the bow. *Edith* plowed through, Jeffrey at the helm, a man fulfilled. He hoped other crews would be at the docks when we came in.

Happy days, but I declined Jeffrey's invitation to work it back up toward home. He said he was going and said when. He said I could work it with him if I wanted to. That was a payout. I didn't get sick anymore and could work it, which counted for plenty later on.

I don't know if a wave broke over the bow at the same moment Brother opened his front door, coming home with his new Mr. Coffee to stash under the sink for when he'd need it. But it could have been, and the split frame put a smile on my face.

Behind the old Mr. Coffee, a new food dehydrator, as seen on TV, had spawned little plastic bags of dehydrated apple slices. New apples and potatoes sat between the dried apples and more plastic bags, hand towels, face towels and paper towels. The counter outlet had two splitters in two plugs and three more plugs in each splitter. A tower of plastic margarine tubs sat beside two radios, mute since '68, the year they carried late-breaking news on Richard Daly and Hubert Humphrey stealing America in Chicago. 1968 was a turning point in the revolution, with long hair, bell-bottoms and more LSD than you could hallucinate a stick at on our side. The warring side was mostly people who wouldn't have to go.

Two cardboard boxes of money-saving coupons ranging from ten to thirty-five cents came next. A deep dig revealed some on the bottom expired twenty years and some still good and worth a try.

Newspaper filled a corner beside another stack of paper bags, and sunrise broke through curtains tacked up ten years prior over old curtains. A cardboard beer case in the Holiday Design sat beside a ninety-gallon trash can. Two beers still waited, holiday varietals.

The old Mr. Coffee squealed and moaned, giving up coffee as begrudgingly as a wino gives blood. I stepped out to the dining room table to sit among the years. In stark contrast, the table was empty, except in the center. I made the butterfly napkin holder in shop in '61. Brother's house was a life archive, an evolutionary record of stuff.

I'd cut out two butterflies, seven-inch wingspan, from quarter-inch plywood on a jigsaw, using the pattern provided in class. I painted both yellow with black trim, my idea. That napkin holder looked silly thirty years later, not so sleek and artistic. Two dowel rods at the bottom wing tips held the butterflies in place, allowing an inch for napkins, but they wobbled, loose. I jimmied matchbook shims into each hole to snug things up and wondered how many other napkin holders had survived from seventh grade shop class of '61. And how many napkin holder makers?

My butterflies got renewed with napkins. It sat beside pot-metal salt and pepper shakers that said Camp Cooke.

Mother was a Girl Scout leader in '55 or '57, when Sissy was a Girl Scout. Spring and fall those years, Troop 38 went up to Camp Cooke for a weekend, and Mother had to take Brother and me because, well, what else could she do? At seven and eight, we couldn't stay home with the old man, lest we fall victim to bologna sandwiches, Orange Crush, chips, beer and tawdry adventures in town. We hadn't yet been clued in on the sex thing, and our little hormones couldn't raise much more than a giggle. We anticipated fun, camping in the woods with none of the pesky ulterior that males suffer from adolescence to last gasp.

Camp fun began on a hike to an old concrete spillway that emptied to a ravine a hundred feet down. A ratty rope hung from a dead limb fifty feet up. Connecting the dots in a blink, the girls shrieked and giggled, and so did Brother and I.

Brother was hefty by then, up to one-fifty and bigger than most girls. He grabbed the rope and walked it back. On a running start, he leapt off the edge to swing way out on a gasp that could have been his last. The limb cracked.

Mother turned to see: Brother was dead meat. But the limb didn't break, and he swung back, scampering onto the ledge just as the rope broke to fall limp, still in his grasp.

She replayed that one for years, staring into space, coming around to remind him what a fool he could be.

She didn't yell too much at the time, and woodland fun filled the day, until the girls got tucked into their cabins for ghost stories in candlelight or pillow fights. Brother and I got tucked into our cot in the big cabin. The five troop leaders weren't nearly as much fun as the girls, but we made the best of it, faking sleep while they undressed. Yakking and slipping out of their dresses and slips, they carried on as if Brother and I were sound asleep and not peeping through eye slits. Down to bras and panties, we simmered to a boil at frightful prospects.

Mrs. Rice, Carol Rice's mother, sensed a murmur, looking over at the two little boys asleep on their cot, and proceeded to peel. Mrs. Rice was old, over thirty, back when exercise was a fringe behavior for eccentric people. Exercise would not have helped Carol Rice's mother, and we didn't care anyway about her shape or privates; we giggled at the principle of the thing. Mrs. Rice was proper to a fault, what we called full o' shit, and busting her naked made the weekend perfect. Our giggle erupted. She shrieked, trying to cover her tits and bush with her hands; too little too late. We laughed out loud, couldn't help it.

Fame and glory would follow us home, but like many returning heroes, we had the horror to bear. Only in private, at home, did we discuss the foreboding thatch Mrs. Rice kept in her panties. It was like any scary thing we knew couldn't really get us and set up more giggles.

Brother kept our high school yearbooks on the dining room table, too, as close as a fresh napkin. Jim Bollinger, sponsor of the High School Writer's Guild in '65, grins stupidly from the yearbook. I didn't join the Writer's Guild, never much of a joiner, and they were too chatty, whacky, zany, confused, unseasoned and most keen on complexity.

Mr. Bollinger was not in the world. He taught English from old lesson plans, not spontaneous but pausing on laugh lines, over-animated, a goofy guy. He gave me As and Bs on compositions the first semester of '64-'65. I liked compositions, even as the other kids groaned, and got an A+ on the final exam, which was another composition, off-the-cuff. Bollinger gave me a B for the semester. "Hey, what?" I asked, report card in hand. His lips twitched, trying for a smile. It went to a frown and another smile, uncertain. He said he wanted to motivate.

I laughed short, motivated to see that it didn't mean shit.

A few weeks later, into second semester and compositions written quickly, Bollinger put *See me!* under a C+. He said I'd stopped trying. I told him he'd failed to motivate. His lips twitched, and we were done.

The next year I drew Mrs. Swope, a scrawny, hook-nosed woman who claimed to be twenty-seven, who sashayed and flirted. Many boys loved the action and played the game. It heated up. I got impatient with silly moves and batty eyes. I liked expository writing, and liking anything was a rarity in school and that phase of life. Mrs. Swope pegged me as a C-, over and over. I could do my best and get a C- or write diddly squat: C-. I thought she acted out her rejection by a senior boy, present and past.

Mrs. Swope assigned a composition on Macbeth. As luck would have it, Sissy had written a Macbeth composition the month before. Also a senior, at Washington University in St. Louis, she got an A+. I copied Sissy's paper verbatim as a control experiment, turned it in and got a C- with a no, no, no and a few K notations in the margins, meaning awkward. Mrs. Swope said no, no, no again when I told her she was not the right teacher for some students, me among them. She condescended over whose place it was to determine appropriateness. Mrs. Swope shook her head on another no, no, no when I showed her Sissy's paper. "I didn't write this paper. My sister did. She's a senior at Washington University majoring in English lit. Wash U is much harder to get into than this high school."

Mrs. Swope looked startled. "You plagiarized your composition?"

"No. I copied it word for word. It got an A+ at Washington University. You gave it a C-. You want to press the issue, that's fine by me. I think we should call in the principal and the English department and the goddamn school board. Or you can transfer me to a new teacher."

She said, "Oh, dear!"

"Yeah," I said.

Mrs. Swope said we should work this out. It would be best.

I told her the work was done. I did it. She would give me As, as warranted, or we would seek a solution. She had failed as a teacher and a woman. Scrawny with a bird beak, she played the vamp, willing to sacrifice others to fill her need. I got transferred to Mrs. Hussong, mid-seventies, thick, slow, challenging and demanding and among the great teachers of history.

Mrs. Hussong taught more on expository composition that year than in all the years prior and graded according to merit.

Mrs. Swope wanted the incident to go away. Giving her the eyeball, head to toe, I shook my head. Cruel, a bit, and just. I was right, pissed off and right. I didn't feel proud but compelled. Maybe justice helped her, too.

Closing the yearbook, I realized how little stuff I'd saved, how little time I took to recollect. If at home in the tropics, I'd get out of bed, brush teeth, take a whiz and a shower, shuffle out to feed the cats and open the door like yesterday. The days lose delineation in life's routine. Midlife can settle like a fog, with doubt and crisis. I felt good most mornings and got stuck in the ooze on others. So?

I'd read that alternate realities cannot be known. At each fork, we choose this way or that. I thought it true, until finding my psychic goggles and seeing the road not taken. I'd come back from many roads to where Mother lived, cooked and worried. That particular return felt different, luminescent and personal. Certain motivation may be regrettable and self-defeating, but I felt the lift. Our family reunion would settle old scores.

A rumble out front of Brother's house took memories to proper proportion. Trash day. The rumble hit 6.5 on the Richter

Scale, coming on. The curtains opened on garbage men slinging hash, whistling, waving and yelling in the stink and tremor as the truck pulled up the driveway past the limits of good taste, the big windshield in spitting distance of the front window.

These guys stood out from the dull commute. Even in razor-sharp cold, they drew flies. The driver chewed a cigar, unlit. He grinned. Just look: at the bottom of the huge windshield, spread open and taped to the glass, a Hustler centerfold showed a woman in gynecological splendor. Dead flies between the page and the glass made for garbage art, garbage truth. Watching his side mirror, he eased back on a whistle and more yelling. "Mo'mbah! Ho! Lep! Rih! Mo'mbah! It woke everyone else in the house, Brother, his parrot and dogs. They screeched and barked.

Squealing brakes and banging trash cans down the street, lids clanging like cymbals, made for a sunrise symphony: The Garbage Sonata. The coachmen had stray maggots on their shoulders, grunge dripping off their gloves, swamp pulp stogies in their teeth.

Brother let the dogs out for a leak, fed the bird, got coffee for himself and, still in his robe on Saturday, shuffled in to turn on the TV. "It's the Smurfs. No talking, please."

Brother became a teacher, inner-city elementary. Father-figure to thirty children, some without fathers, colleague to thirty teachers who knew about white people; oh yeah.

Maybe he was back in third grade to set things straight, just as Mrs. Swope had returned to high school. I visited once. He introduced me to his third-graders as Ronald Reagan, President of the United States of America. He explained aside that these children would not likely be exposed to powerful men otherwise.

The children were impressed and wanted to know, "Where's Nancy?"

"She's had a headache since last night," I said. "Don't you worry. The wealth and promise of America will trickle down to you, too."

They wanted to know when, and why not now, and where's the ice cream, you honky fucker?

Brother laughed. His kids laughed, too, and consensus prevailed. He understood these kids in the same bizarre way they got his twisted method. He taught life uniquely, in a way they would feel. Over the years, he met former kids at regular intervals. As adults, they smiled with sanguine perspective on teaching, insight and irony.

Brother was copping smokes in the garage by eighth grade, a year after the split. Prior years had been harder for him. He didn't like to fish and wouldn't go. He'd eat it if he had to but didn't want to.

The old man gave him a fishing rod and a box of lures for his tenth birthday; time to grow up and fish like a man.

Brother cried, unacceptable behavior to the old man, who was not always the cavalier rogue I perceived.

At times rough, mean, drunk and disagreeable, the old man could vent failures and frustrations on anyone. He yelled about crybabies, getting out and not being so goddamn fat your whole life. Sensing his error, maybe, he yelled that none of us were worth the powder to blow us up, for chrissake.

The unromantic, irrational, often cruel side had reasoned fishing tackle as the perfect gift for Brother, fishing tackle long awaiting an excuse to blow the money on it.

He smacked Brother, a backhand, a light one. It didn't hurt much, nothing like a Socko paddle spanking for really fucking up, like wrecking the hose bibs outside so the water ran all day, and the place looked like a houseboat. We got blistered asses for that one and lay whimpering in late afternoon as the ducks quacked happily outside, as yelling and shrieking reached new heights down the hall.

"Wait until I tell your father," Mother had said when the water began to rise. When he got home, she told him. He whipped us with a Socko paddle. She screamed bloody murder, called him a lunatic and called the cops. He split downtown for a drink, after showing her what any fucking idiot ought to know: the shut-off valve. An easy twist turned off the water. She cursed him out the driveway for expecting her to know what no man would take a lousy minute to show her.

But the fishing-tackle, birthday-backhand left an imprint.

Everything got back to normal, such as it was. Brother put a brave face on his decision to kill the old man. A Milk of Magnesia every night would ensure a good shit in the morning, to ditch the steak and fried chicken that otherwise got stuck. The old man's habit called for the giant Milk of Magnesia, the blue bottle so big, he wouldn't notice two ounces of iodine added. This was '57 or '58, when iodine had skull and crossbones on the label.

Brother had focus. This mission would take balls, like Jack up the Beanstalk trying to steal the giant's harp. Jack or Brother

159

could die trying. We got home at three. He slipped into the bathroom just after the old man got home at three oh five, while I mixed a highball. He dumped the iodine into the Milk of Magnesia, shook it up and came out poker-faced.

He stayed scarce six hours, sweating it out when the old man hit the bathroom to pour a long one. Brother figured that was it, the old man would be dead by morning, and he'd go to reform school and prison forever.

He drifted to sleep about four, but we woke up about five to a thunderous shitstorm in the bathroom. Brother breathed easier, as he and the old man got a load off. Good moods abounded that sunrise. The old man didn't click his heels or sing *Zip-a-Dee-Doo-Dah* but smiled on a half nod here and there.

Brother and I got up early and went out to play, and the old man didn't die for another three or four years.

Brother is a vegetarian now.

Above the cardboard box collection, near the hutch in the formal dining room, hanging on the wall in a corner was the photo gallery dedicated to me. An eight-by-ten shows me at twenty on a motorcycle with a goatee, sunglasses and a jacket from Goodwill: Profile in Arrogance. It's deadpan, like Marlon Brando in *The Wild Bunch* but more uncertain. It's from a high-speed summer in Europe, shot in the Alps after a blowout on a medium curve at sixty. Death got cheated those days. I smirked, fearful but alive and willing to go again, proving something or other. Young enough to fix the flat and ride four hours more over a frozen pass, where another shot showed more arrogance, we stopped near the summit to grasp hot pipes in ragtag gloves to thaw finger joints. We didn't take no shit from no fucking Alps.

The next shot profiles more fear, this time with humility, tripping hard on a bummer. Intro to the Face of God was not a college course, but we learned. Overdosed and unclean, that acid had strychnine. Rushes were in, and bad acid couldn't kill, really, most of the time.

Next in the gallery is a three-shot of Lester, Moonpie and me in sunny Florida. It looks like good times, with a Porsche and a motor yacht, sunshine and palm trees. In '79, Moonpie and I went down from Charleston, South Carolina, a town with no present tense, pickled in Scotch, numbed out and decked out in flowers like a wake, until cocaine hit like defibrillators on a flat graph. That woke 'um up.

Lester was the man. He flew down for the photo-op.

Moonpie and I drove the Porsche.

Lester had been holing up at my place. Sue had left, soon to be the ex-wife. I was broke, unemployed and unemployable. I told Lester he could stay, not that he asked. He showed up with groceries, beer, sometimes women, all the time drugs and took the guest room. I had none of the above, except for the guest room. What could I say, no? I told him he could stay with a recreational stash but no pounds or kilos. He said that was smart and the cardinal rule of survival in the drug trade. Job security required three places: a place for the stash, a place for the cash, a place to crash. A dealer's biggest worry is getting busted: cops or crooks. If he's with his stash and his cash, he's a three-time loser.

With geographic diversity, he can make bail and deal another day.

He'd said he could use a smart guy, if a guy wanted to work. He'd been talking about renegades in Florida who ran speedboats out to mother ships to off-load drugs and run back in, making a hundred grand in a month.

I'd never imagined a hundred grand. Sure, I'd work, I'd been on boats, had a career on a shrimp boat, kind of.

As a lawyer and CPA, Lester got bored. He laughed, "You study the law and crunch numbers for hours and days; you gonna get bored." He dealt cocaine to liven things up and make more money. He knew the business, having worked his way through law school dealing reefer. He dealt cocaine in ounces, mostly, cut from kilos he bought from Columbians in South Florida, where they kept warehouses of it. They wanted Lester to run a warehouse. Lester said no, he just wanted to work it on the mom 'n pop level. I think they scared him, until a bunch of Cubans killed the Colombians with machine guns and ruled South Florida; until a new bunch of Colombians killed the Cubans with machine guns and took back what was rightfully theirs.

A kilo went about twenty grand then. Ounced out at a grand per, a kilo rolled over for fifteen grand on the plus side, *mas o menos*. Lester averaged a pound a week, and demand was steady. This was way before crack and gangs and epidemic drug abuse, back when cocaine dealers were lovable outlaws. Maurice Chevalier was a guest on Johnny Carson about then and recalled his days as a prisoner of war in WW I, when the world and humanity were more genteel. He got wistful over the prison guards who offered cocaine daily, for the social grace of it. "Ah, but nev-eh more than one or two sniffs per day." Then he sang, "The birds in the trees seem to whisper Louise. Ah love you."

About that time, a big bust went down near Charleston on a guy who'd come up the dealer ranks from the auto-assembly line, where he sold reefer, so the work could be numb as well as mindless. He'd formed a distribution network in the Southeast, until he got popped with twelve tons of reefer on three shrimp trawlers. All on board got arrested, separated and told that the others had made deals with the prosecution.

Outside organization got critical in a hurry, so a slew of lawyers came in to assure the defendants that no deals had been made. Lester maneuvered to become counsel for the kingpin, who faced twenty years in the federal slammer in Atlanta.

The kingpin had been importing long enough to make a load o' dough and parlay it into real estate, boats, cars and so on, all in his mother's or girlfriend's name.

Once the boys made bail, it was high times in town. They couldn't leave and had no recourse but to ship in enough drugs to sustain legal defense and good times till the trial. I was included, Lester's landlord and a smart guy and all. Everybody was best of friends, happy to be alive, shaking hands and tootin' it up, making plays for women who didn't mind, as long as the toot held out. It was good times, as seen on TV, like at the Playboy mansion, loud and coarse.

Lester got the kingpin to hand over his get-away car keys after the trial. That was the black Porsche, refitted with crazy engines to scream, even on a grocery run. If Lester had it, it couldn't be impounded. Well, it could, but they'd never find him.

Lester drove fast all over town, working out the details on his fiduciary trust: real estate liquidation on the kingpin's assets to generate cash for legal defense up the appeals chain. The kingpin would need money win or lose; life is spendy, and the Big House takes steady dough to keep an asshole intact.

Liquifiable assets included twenty acres of rocky scrub in Central Kentucky, hardly worth a shit, much less the fifty grand he'd paid for it in the glory days, when he and his band of merry men wanted a landing strip in the Midwest. They'd sent a young renegade to do the deal, and he'd flashed the cash with outlaw spirit. Local yokels lowered their eyes and said thank you and called the Feds. That's how the empire crumbled.

A year later I went to Central Kentucky, via Lester, attorney for the defense. Lester gave me some credit cards and a hundred bucks for road stuff. Suddenly mobile, flush and employed, I sensed a future at last. Lester said if I could get ten grand for the Kentucky property, he'd give me a grand, which was the difference between penniless and a thousand dollars. Lester said don't worry about title complexities; he'd work it out in escrow. He was a lawyer, after all.

"How you do-een? Eddie N. Deep. Eddie N. Deep Century 21." Eddie N. Deep wore the piss-yellow blazer of a Century 21 associate. "Com-puter linked with fourteen-thousand Century 21 associates worldwide." He offered his hand, saying the field was worthless but for holding the state record on rattlesnakes per acre.

"Ah shitchu not." He said an auction would be best. "Auction draws 'm out, don't you know."

I told him I needed ten grand. He said, "Shit. Ain't nobody knows what she'll bring. They all be there, but everybody knows about the rocks and rattlesnakes. Shit."

The auction was set for one, just after dinner. Eddie banged the gavel and called for a bid, any bid, and finally got one for five grand. Everybody laughed. Eddie N. Deep said he'd have to take this unrealistic offer to the owner for advisement. Everybody looked at me.

I shrugged.

On the flight home I wondered if the deal would fly, and if I'd get my five hundred on the sale.

I flew south a week later to the Bahamas to sell seventy acres. If I could get fifty grand, I could keep three. I'd advertised in Germany, *Die Velt*, and in France, *Le Monde*, via the *Wall Street Journal* and its translation service. Lester paid for that, too.

I got letters from the Sultan of Oman and a few Germans and invited everyone down to Eleuthera for a showing. The Sultan couldn't make it, but the Germans did. They wanted to buy it but wouldn't go into escrow without seeing the title. I told them that's what escrow does, gets the title from the seller.

"*Nein!*"

I called Lester. He said I'd done good; he'd take it from there, come on home. He had another assignment.

I hung out a few days on Eleuthera, maybe scratching an old itch, making the tropics at last. I watched the local boys chum sharks with chicken guts, setting a grappling hook with a whole chicken on a towline off the back of a rental jeep. They hooked a hammerhead who dragged the jeep into the hubs, till the guy at the wheel saw that the shark was bigger than the jeep and stronger than 4-wheel drive and cut his losses along with the polypropylene towline.

Club Med was just down the beach, so I eased in and met a woman from Venezuela. She agreed that the place wasn't real and came back to my motel for some barbecued chicken and funky chicken, and I was broke again. I wanted to stay and hang out with the Bahamians who danced by the pool every night. They laughed at me, a white guy with moves, like lumpy syrup on a downbeat. I wanted to linger in the sensuality in those days of no AIDS, long ago. Those people understood the spirit of fun that doesn't cost much, but I had much less and had to go home.

The new assignment was driving the getaway car to South Florida with Moonpie, Lester's little brother, whose disposition was more like a cowpie with a lit firecracker stuck in it. Moonpie plain didn't mind splattering shit all over the place; fuck you and yer fuckin' bullshit, motherfucker.

Lester said, "Here," handing over the Porsche keys and four hundred-dollar bills that only recently seemed like a bankroll but spent very fast. I suspected manipulation to keep me broke, so I'd have to run home to run more errands. I didn't complain. Along with the money were two guns, .38s, so Moonpie and I could shoot our way out, if we ran out of money.

"Why do we need guns?"

"Don't worry," Lester said. "You ain't carrying."

"Yeah, well, why guns?"

He grinned. "Moonpie likes guns. He needs two. You know, in case one runs outa ammo."

Moonpie giggled, firing off a few rounds, two-fisted, until Lester yelled, "Not here!"

Moonpie frowned. Lester was so bossy, always yelling what Moonpie couldn't do.

Moonpie cheered up a few days later, when Lester sent him to parachute school over at the airfield in Savannah, part of a new strategy. Lester was big on technology and orchestration. He thought best to bypass the Colombians and Cubans and other Latin maniacs shooting each other up for turf control. He couldn't trust any of them to set him up with a load and not turn him in to get rid of him.

It made no sense. Why set him up to turn him in? Why not just shoot him? I asked.

Lester looked at me like I was dumb as Moonpie.

Moonpie giggled, ready to jump.

Lester's plan would eliminate the mother ship, the courier boats, the crews and drivers and all the stuff that could go bad. The plan was simple: get the cocaine packed flat, inch-thick slabs, and duct-tape it to Moonpie's back and chest. Fuck yeah, you shave it first.

"Oh, fuck it," Moonpie giggled, "Just shave and tape that shit all over." Moonpie loved the action and thought his brother was a wizard and trusted his brother to take care of him. After a crash course in parachuting, he got a flight to Colombia and bought sixty pounds of cocaine and got a pilot to fly him back over South Florida at night, low. Without landing, the airplane couldn't be arrested without a dogfight, and at night, Moonpie would be invisible. He jumped at three thousand feet with three seconds easy to gather his wits, pull his cord and not die.

He said later he kind of fucked up, snooting so much of the stuff beforehand, you know, for the rush. It kind of messed up his timing, you know, and then all that spinning and dark bullshit. He missed his pickup point by a mile or so and had to slog through the swamps and was scared to death of alligators and snakes and shit, but he made it okay.

Lester gave him three grand credit on what he owed for parachute school, liquor and toot, which got his debt down to eight grand. Moonpie said that felt a whole lot better than eleven grand.

Meanwhile, with Florida postponed two weeks, I was two weeks penniless.

Lester said sorry, he didn't have no money, since I fucked up in the Bahamas. I smelled bullshit, but he came back quick, before I could ask who fucked up what.

He said, "If you want to . . ."

If I wanted to, I could run down to Hilton Head Island with five ounces he hadn't been able to move, to see how I could do, gramming it out. He'd front me a hundred bucks along with the toot and wouldn't do that for anybody but me.

"You put your nose in the bag, you pay for it." He laughed, "You might break even. Gram dealers fall into the bag often as not."

I was to head out that night, because drug dealers work at night. I made a few calls for market research, and yes, the market was strong on Hilton Head Island. I spent the next few hours weighing grams and packing bindles, going to eight-balls—three point five for the price of three—for efficiency and diversity.

Around ten p.m., seeing me out the door, Lester said, "Three places. Stash, cash and crash."

I said I'd heard that before.

Well, even a country Jew can't head down the road on a trip like that without a headful of Mother, gnashing teeth and wringing hands and a big talk bubble full of *Oy Vay*! My son, the toot man. The old man, who surfaced on new projects, would have cleaned my clock, but . . . maybe not, having reckoned a few needs of his own between a shit and a sweat. This was '78 or '79, seventeen years since he'd checked out but way before all the athletes and great guys dropped dead from too much toot.

You shudder, looking back on what you thought was spirited youth. I got lucky, taunting phantoms in a fool's paradise, surviving what some friends did not.

I got down to Hilton Head Island about midnight, just as the clubs were finding high gear. In ten minutes, the market found me, was throwing cash at me, demanding goods and services. I applied my degree and slowed way down to ask a friend if I could keep a bag at his house and ask another friend if I could keep another bag at her house. That was stash and cash taken care of, so I split to settle most of the stash and worked it an hour to one, not even brunch time for the night people. I stashed the cash, got more stash and got back to work. As for crash: forget it.

A sweet young thing looked right through me to what she wanted and knew she could get it. She looked like Daisy Mae and came on strong. I wanted to take her home, her home, but she smiled sweetly and said no, let's drink and dance some more. She murmured softly, "Relax, will you? We'll fuck all night if you want to, but I want to hang out here for a while first and dig this buzz. Geez, you act like you're married. You are, aren't you?" I shrugged it off, shagged her a drink and gave her a line. Just that quick, it didn't matter if I was a novitiate at the monastery. Besides, I was separated by then, but a cool breeze knows better than to explain things.

Drug dealers were romantic characters then, outlaws who knew about romance on the fly, down to friction on modified consciousness. Love is rarely without problems, needs and the endless play of give and take. By the time we got back to her place, I was feeling way past due. Honoring her pledge, she went to everyman's fantasy, coming up to complain about guys always wanting the same thing and acting like big babies when they didn't get it on time. I felt wrongly accused but nodded agreement. I knew this line of work could not develop into a career, but the job interview made a big impression.

I called Daisy Mae for a while after that, but she was out. I heard later that she found Jesus. Lucky Him.

Meanwhile, I sold four ounces, grammed out. I brought one home and turned enough cash to pay for inventory, drinks and gas and had fifty bucks left.

Lester said, "It's hell, ain't it?"

The next week, Moonpie and I drove south in the getaway car with our four bills and two guns. Moonpie hated being passed, and when a cocksucker in a fucking Saab, of all the chickenshit cars, passed us doing a hundred-five, he whimpered. He stomped on it, reaching under his seat for a gun, cheek to steering wheel, weaving at one-thirty.

"Jesus Christ, Moonpie."

"I got it. I got it." He was only going to shoot the guy in the Saab if we couldn't pass him. We did.

I didn't ask if he planned to roll down the window for the shot. He would have taken it as a challenge. He said, "Turbo. Big motherfucking deal. Cocksuckers. Saabs. Ha!"

Lester waited dockside in Ft. Liquordale, as we called it. He'd flown down. He said, "You keep it," when I offered three fifty in change on the road cash. I said thanks, but I'd earned it and knew he was priming my pump again. Let him.

Moonpie parked the Porsche by Lester's new yacht, as a woman who looked about thirty going on fifty came off the yacht like a robot on basic programing.

She walked out front, aimed a camera at us and whined, "Smi-ull." She told us to bunch up so she could get the car in there, too. I turned away, so I could explain later, your honor, I had no idea what was going on down there. And there I hang on Brother's wall, looking away. I swiped the film that night, of course, when I saw the camera on a shelf in the main cabin. The world was a simpler place before digital and phone cameras.

The yacht also belonged to the kingpin. We drank and tooted on board a day and a night, and Lester laid out the plan. He'd heavily insured the vessel. It didn't take a career criminal to see that one coming. He figured the best way was to run the bitch hard aground in the entrance channel at low tide. With enough speed, she'd run up on the sandbar in the center. The tide came in fast there with five-foot breakers on the sandbar to break her up quick, if we could fracture the hull on impact. The fire would finish it, once we lit the gasoline poured over the decks.

Moonpie twitched for the fun of it.

I sat back.

Lester said, "Moonpie'll do all the work. You just tag along, jump off when he says jump off and swim in with him."

I was still on heavy current and big breakers but asked, "What makes you think Moonpie'll know when to jump off?"

"You'll be there," he said, smiling, and I knew he loved his brother after all, or at least he knew good help like Moonpie would be hard to replace. "Ten grand," he said, just like he'd said a grand over Kentucky and three grand over Eleuthera. I was right around four hundred bucks up since then, after breaking enough federal laws to get a few lifetimes up the river. I said I wanted to walk around the block and stretch out some.

Lester smiled his weak smile, the disappointed one that said *You can't run, because I'll find you.* I caught a taxi to the airport a few blocks down and bought a ticket home, cash. That was the last I saw of Moonpie and Lester.

Moonpie went alone and lived to talk about it. The boat they trashed was fifty years old in perfect condition. Lester settled for thirty grand on the claim.

About six months later, I got a call from another smuggler, a friendly guy I'd met on the social circuit. We'd hit it off. He said a man in a pinstripe suit and a new Lincoln with rental plates just dropped in, asking about me and Lester. The man worked for the kingpin. They were looking for Lester, who'd tried to steal the kingpin's assets. "I told him you're a dumb shit," the guy on the phone said. "Told him you didn't know nothing but running errands for Lester."

I said thank you and meant it and that the profile was accurate. I woke up about three a.m. in front of test patterns, where I'd fallen asleep on the couch, stiff, waiting for the guy in a suit. He never showed. I knew those guys, mean and aggressive with low-level speech patterns, a crude, go-for-it mentality and a keen sense of revenge. Not romantic renegades but lowlifes who measured machismo in dollars, they attracted women weak for cocaine. They had a hard time building sentences but maimed easy for a grand, killed for ten, and Lester had fucked the kingpin out of three hundred-thousand.

I don't know if the old man brought any influence to bear on the guy in the pinstripe suit, if a certain brain wave got bent just right, half a degree in another direction. Maybe he did. That was '79. Maybe he rearranged a few molecules in the bad acid choking me to death ten years earlier, so I wouldn't have to get busted at the hospital and have Mother remind me for the next thirty years. Maybe he kept my back wheel straight, on the road, when it blew out, or had a hand in letting the chains fall off my ankle so I wouldn't drown. I don't know, but I wonder at the long odds on the long stretch of close calls over the years.

I don't think I got arrogant or felt immortal. Surviving a near miss on going down for good left me drenched in fear every time. But I wondered: can a protective spirit alter events?

Like with Satan, the marsh stallion who let me slip a bridle over his head and swing a leg over his back and ease on up, before making it clear as the clear blue sky that it'd be him or me that day. I'd walked across the pasture from the trailer Sue and I rented cheap, because money was short in shrimping time—walked across to where Marie and Jack discussed whether Satan would be better off as glue.

"Can I ride him?"

They looked up. "You can try," Jack said.

I'd seen guys ride bareback on TV, and it was only ten years since I was going to be a champion jockey. I jumped on, all set to kiss Satan with my knees, but he tore out for a limb so low it scraped his neck and would have scraped me off his back. I'd seen Indians on TV hang off the blind side so the cowboys couldn't shoot them. That was easy. Getting back up wasn't so easy, until Satan sideswiped the barn. I got back up, never mind my leg mashed into the barn—it was only severely bruised and a better sacrifice than my head. We had a rough stalemate into the bucking phase, before Satan picked up steam, before he dropped through the trapdoor, leaving me nothing to hold on to, then shot out like a cannonball.

I bailed, let go and flew off. Satan hung a right and ran eight miles to the beach where he would have tried to drown me.

I watched him go, lying in the dirt, bloody and dizzy, asking Jack and Marie, "Why didn't you tell me?"

"Tell you what?" Jack asked.

Maybe the old man put a pinch on Satan's ear or backed up tall Paul K five years later when he reached over the rail and grabbed my ankle to haul me back aboard as the lifeline broke. I'd stood on it to reach a tangle in the main sheet at the boom end, twenty miles out in eight-foot seas on a cold, gray day, racing to Savannah.

I don't know and don't know if it was sheer blind luck, surviving another crossing in the Pacific with thirty-foot waves breaking overhead and fifty knots of breeze that beat the crew to a whimper and a grunt, beyond hope on a night that won't die.

I think people who lose parents early, especially kids from the hell-bent-for-leather school who lose fathers in the crux of puberty, on the threshold of immortality, sense the spirit more naturally. Childish wonder may also linger, as a basis for denial. Or a parent checking out too soon may hover longer, as necessary, until the kid gets seasoned. For years I felt assisted in crunch times. An ethereal presence made for calmness, which is key in the clutch. Nobody cried at the old man's funeral, because he'd shown them the heavy hand, but when I cried, all cried for the kid with no father. Compensating for the loss among us, they laid hands on each other and me. Everyone crying changed the tenor and flow, setting things up for memory and reflection.

Who knows about guardian spirits? I don't, but the time stands out in a room full of the old man, soon after he was dead and buried, in the lingering interval for many spirits. Time came down to the split-second when Flossie's son raised his hand against me, and I didn't poke another bean but flicked my wrist, just so, bringing the fork up in a convergence of fingers, wrist, heart and head, to impale the aggressor. I still ponder the strength required to penetrate a forearm with a fork.

That was thirty years prior, and the problem persisted with a warm tingle, head to toe. Goose bumps sprouted as tines broke skin, seeking height and depth.

VI

BLIND FAITH

I only know what Mother told of early childhood. Recollection comes as snapshots, short on context or continuity, like getting a bath in the sink, a perfect fit, with Mother keeping me afloat and laughing at my splashing, amazed at my amazing skill. Or a coonskin cap like Davy Crockett's or flannel jammies with a pooper flap and built-in mukluks. I opened the front door on Brother coming home from school, and wondered over Mother's excitement, dressing me as a girl for Halloween.

She said I looked for danger, climbing what could be climbed, a difficult child in need of watching. She said I made her look bad, age five, dinner with the Meadrikes, the lovely new neighbors. We'd just moved in, and she'd wanted to make an impression. I stood on a chair, so cute, pulled out my dick and said, "Look at this!"

Mother didn't call it a dick; she called it a *shmeckel*, soft-form Yiddish for shmuck, and told the story, lest we forget. "I was mortified."

"Are you still mortified?"

She thought it over. She nodded.

"Let's call the Meadrikes," I suggested.

"And say what? You're sorry?"

"No. We'll just say hello and make nice, the way you like."

"They died," she said. "That was forty years ago."

"You're saying that time can heal, after all?"

She stared off, at time, and said I never let her rest as an infant, sticking fingers into sockets, crossing streets, headstrong at three, bringing home rats and snakes, barehanded. Tippy caught them. I brought them in for safekeeping.

Unacceptable behaviors formed a pattern, survivor. Scrappy and willful are harsh parameters from infant innocence to formative youth. Mother let it be known: I lacked discipline from a man. I thought survival had both required and reflected a winning effort. The college years helped, with recreational drugs to diffuse floating hostilities, and I fit in at last with the other kids.

I didn't attend college graduation, such a hollow exercise. For years I couldn't claim graduation from the state U because of loans waiting payment. They wanted the money and threatened sincerely, with phrases like "your permanent record" or "doing the right thing." In time, they couldn't find me.

I rationalized not paying, having learned rationale in college, where we bunkered against the jungle war, a federal incursion of

Viet Nam for material gain. We couldn't stay in college unless the Feds loaned the money. That's extortion, a loan scam. Borrow the money, or hit the swamps. Many other guys went. Some survived and came home to comprise the biggest segment of Viet Nam war protestors.

Rationale could be sophistry, another lesson learned in the humanities, but in this case it wasn't. The oblique objective was "Democracy," though we saw resource allocation as the prime motive and thought no bottom line could rationalize the body count. History and contemporary Viet Nam prove the point.

The state U mailed my college degree in Creative Writing to Mother. She hung it over the TV then married twice more, moved south and back north and way south and back up to Flossie's place, so it could hang over Brother's TV. It's dated 1970 and certifies successful avoidance of the jungle war, the war that bolstered the academic/medical complex, requiring college to avoid the war, then requiring medical proof of unacceptability for war.

The choice was clear: reefer, acid and Intro to Sexual Revolution 101, or hot swamps, diseases, snakes, landmines and smallish strangers shooting to kill. Oh, and leeches, mosquitoes and first lieutenants. It didn't take a college degree to figure that one. Decadent fun did not justify the waste of time, but college in the 60s was a rare entry to reality outside the norm, outside of self, stoned as a way of being, replacing ambition with alternatives, with meaningful connection for a better journey.

Besides the jungle war, I factored Social Security benefits. The old man died years earlier, after a life of minimal payments to the system. The government, those same pesky Feds, albeit a different agency, sent $140 monthly to college students under twenty-two whose deceased parents had paid in, if the kid stayed in college. With four years on that dole, I had it dicked. Rent: thirty-five bucks. New-car payment: forty-five (VW bug with peace symbols). With groceries at thirty-five, that left thirty clams a month for draft beer at twenty-five cents and decent Mexican lids at twelve bucks. Of course, it's never enough, and cash got tight a few days shy of month's end.

With pocket dough, fun could be a way of life. Drugs and liquor made college an easy choice over swamps, bullets and sundry madness. Wasting time in college was a lesser of two evils. College was not death, where far more time can be wasted. College kids then, especially in the arts, had snug harbor, never mind the bullshit buffoonery; what a beautiful backdrop for stagnation, reflection and discussion.

The degree in Creative Writing for sale at the University of Missouri required eight short stories written in the fourth year, about one a month, which didn't inconvenience the social opportunities at hand. Student writers could develop their artistry in story critiques among peers, a figurative blood bath among egotistical, moderately talented persons, some of whom cried on hearing the cruel truth.

The first three years required forty forgettable courses that fit well in the hallucination of those days. One stand-out: *17th Century Metaphysical Poetry and Prose.* Professor Bowtie seethed on aggressively modest demeanor, small stature, cheap suits with vests and bowties for singularity. His name is lost, but his voice survives, slowing time to slag and drool, like two Seconals and a tallboy and all the world down from 78 to 33 1/3. I attended two classes, first and last. The rest were easily imagined.

Day 1 was traditional, checking it out for chicks, goofs, laughs. First days were ritual, semesters marking time in four-month increments, as the academic bunker eroded like sandstone in a breeze. The Bible grants three score and ten years; the university gave eight semesters. Hot swamps waited.

First days seemed happy and grim, like a New Orleans funeral, horns and dancing, surreal and consequential. Everybody dies someday, but it wouldn't be that day or at any time in a hundred twenty more days. We passed courses to survive.

The war seemed ambient, a presence among us. Ag students right off the farm in 4-H jackets came to the state U to refine their techniques, working to keep America fed.

Long-hairs, rag-tag and rolling joints at the Student Commons, loved to ask an aggie for a light. These days, the aggies get high like everybody, but not then.

What a laugh.

The last day of class was the final exam, four months later. A composition bluebook was twenty-five cents at the U Book Store. I picked one up on the way and walked in stone cold but stoned enough for confidence.

Choose 3 of the following 6, the final exam said, *for comparison intrinsically to each other and/or themselves and/or to a single iota of the real world,* or some shit. *Please annotate.* The 6 were 17th Century metaphysical poets, must have been. I sat there thinking, *Ho boy*, scratching my nuts. *Please scrotate*, I wrote on the final, but this was no time to choke; the hot swamp waited, burbling with creepy crawlies and larvae that could swim up a pee hole, teeming humidity and the itch cloying for instant resolution in the tick . . . tick . . . tick . . . stillness of that stuffy room, where reality refugees hunched over bluebooks to spew bullshit to gain another four months.

I had no choice, surrounded, do or die; take the bold move, make a break and run for cover, swerving, ducking, rolling, veering for the clear. Or fold in the clutch and . . .

Move out, soldier!

Do you solemnly swear . . .

I shined the question as written. Fuck 3; I never heard of these guys. I decided to pick one and wail. Andrew Marvell. I remember: it would be such a marvel that I'd fill a bluebook on his life, his work, his intrinsicality to himself. I compared the works of Andrew Marvell to *Bonanza*, showing how Hoss Cartwright, Little Joe, Lorne Green, Shoo Fly and Frog Dick were, in fact, practically, if not pragmatically, intrinsically, possibly, potentially, innately linked one and the same to the overriding theme and/or motif of Marvell's dominant love-hate, or, rather, approach-avoidance processing of poetry, or, as far as we know, of prose, too, after all.

I filled the bluebook. That was the main thing, especially getting down to the last two pages where cursive writing must shrink so the important stuff can get crammed in. It wasn't bad. I used the episode of Bonanza from the night before to compare and contrast, still fresh, a bit clouded with hash smoke, sure, but mere hours old. A few friends had gathered to watch with ice cream, pizza, cookies, pickles, beer, soda, chips, the usual. In deference to finals week, psychedelic drugs went on hold. It wasn't like we were completely irresponsible.

I got a C-.

Professor Bowtie understood. If I had to waste four years, it wasn't his fault, and if he had to waste time on students forced into college, well . . . Whatever. The vast majority of campus population was anti-war, except for the ROTC guys, though many of them signed up to stay out of combat and came home to join the movement.

A big lesson in college, or a lesson clearly demonstrated in those anxious days, was that only those who commit to risk can win or lose. The rest stay lukewarm in a life of purgatory, cradle to grave.

Many smart people never went to college. Many suspect they'd be smarter if they'd gone. But no college teaches smarts— no university, law or med school. That's why most of them test for admission, to see who's already smart. They teach information and method. They don't teach common sense, much less wisdom. Smart people acquire those things on their own, often at a much earlier age than college students.

I learned the truth of writing fiction from Ted Moffett, a teaching assistant and writer who taught Narration 50. Ted was the real deal, a guy who didn't want to be a writer but had to be a writer, a guy who thought about character, plot and flow all the time, a guy whose marriage came second, like the rest of his life.

Narration 50 was a prerequisite for Short Story 404, where the student writer would write short stories under the tutelage of William Heyden, fiction heavyweight.

Bill Heyden was not a great writer or a good writer. He'd been an editor at *Story* magazine. He also grew in stature from the legend mill that churned silly shit on campus. Bill Heyden did not give first breaks to Ernest Hemingway, Scott Fitzgerald, John Steinbeck or any legendary name. Bill Heyden was not heavy. But the mill churned and spewed. Students drank beer, smoked dope and believed that silly shit. That was campus life.

Not a bad guy, Professor Heyden spoke with an affected Vuhginia accent, his tutelage in a nutshell: "We are here. We have, shall we say, certain requirements (ruh•KWAH•munts). Now. Let us proceed." He sounded like, shall we say, Foghorn Leghorn, subdued and polished but not as poignant. I learned nothing, in alignment with the unwritten curriculada.

Ted Moffett, on the other hand, was a fiction heavy, unknown, unheralded, unimposing, a workhorse who honed and developed, buffed and burnished, reflected and went again. Ted Moffett had no past, no money to speak of, no prospects beyond the bottle and blind faith that one day his writing would entertain and uplift, his audience would grow, his stories endure. At twenty-nine in '68, old already, he didn't mind drinking with students, getting drunk on occasion and talking about writing, no punches pulled, no niceties necessary. He had a beard and could hold his liquor and, most importantly, underscored the good things in his students' stories, touched on the weak parts, what needed fixing, maybe a few things to consider. He worked on his writing every day and said, "I don't know," when he didn't know.

Ted Moffett knew what he liked and didn't like. As a stylist, a nitty gritty man at ground level, he reflected and took insight to his writing. He avoided the voice common to campus writers. He moved apart from academic burdens, ditching the ponderous and imposing otherness of narration. He was to Bill Heyden like Vincent Van Gogh was to Peu Peu Pierre.

My college short stories, dusty but not too moldy, sat on top of Brother's dining room hutch. I leafed through, browsing the detritus of a cloudy young mind. Tuition and grades, war anxiety and social upheaval, cerebral machination and delusion framed those stories. A random page dealt with a twenty-one-year-old boy meeting an exotic woman of thirty-five. Another dealt with a man who took drugs and got morose and went insane.

In my last year, '69-'70, the Selective Service lottery was also known as War Bingo, though the game came closer to Russian roulette. The drawing was televised, prime time, with 366 ping-pong balls, each with a birth date, drawn from a fishbowl by an old man in a rumpled suit. We watched, smoking joints, drinking liquor.

Near the end of that year and Short Story 404, Bill Heyden began in tedious drawl, aristocratic as his fictional character, so saying very little took a while: "I want you all to consider the Ph.D." He paused, as if silence was drama. "Some of you won't know what to do at matriculation." He hinted comprehension of our recent waste of time and the coming predicament. "Most important of all is the serious commitment to fiction. You will either make it or not make it." He said we'd reached the age of playing for keeps, and a commitment to fiction would include the Ph.D. "Eighty percent of all National Book Award winners hold the Ph.D."

Who had room in his cerebellum for considering the Ph.D.? College had its high times, but more years of textbook reality could stunt growth on a permanent basis. Then again, a college graduate in a soft art is a prime candidate for grunt labor. The jungle war beckoned, so maybe the Ph.D. would be best, in San Francisco, while awaiting the trial for refusing induction.

College students love two birds, one stone, figuratively speaking. A graduate teaching job would pay, likely more than Social Security benefits to fatherless college kids under twenty-two. By teaching six hours a week while taking courses and crafting a dissertation, a grad student might defer reality and squeeze another three years through the wringer, maybe four. Deferral could not be confused with deferment, but campus still seemed snug.

Two other heavyweights rounded out the writing faculty at the state U in Mid-Mo, two poets who could have been late forties but looked mid-sixties from liquor and Camel straights. One was shaped like a hippopotamus, with massive flesh in folds on a tired hulk and a puffy face. He'd won awards and, though slovenly as a poet, enjoyed esteem on campus, which was better than derision.

I had the other one for Poetry 402. Long, skinny, bedraggled Tom McAfee had also risen to celebrity status among the intellectual cadre, such as it was, at a state U best known for its ag school. Affable Tom McAfee was a great poet and decent guy, perhaps more likable with no awards, indifferent as a poet should be to the concept of awards or competition in an art form. Students read their poems in his class, while he hunched over a smoke, shoulders stooped, sometimes nodding, sometimes smiling halfway, sometimes laughing short, prelude to a long drag and exhale, animating truth with insight. His pack of smokes always looked empty, yet he could drag one more fag from the crumple.

Tom McAfee never spoke to me directly but addressed one of my poems on the floor. "That should be I wish I were there." He puffed and shook his head. "Not I wish I was there."

I call it: "Still Life at State U."

Professor McAfee drank coffee and smoked more cigarettes at the Student Commons, usually with the philosophy guys, but he stayed clear of their tirades and semaphores over sequential causality of events in precognizant yet post-deliberate series— yes, series, not single events, because how can a single event be?

Or some shit.

He watched, smoked, hunched and half-laughed. Or was that a cough? I couldn't ask him what he thought about the Ph.D. He was busy, thinking on a poem about nothingness, decay, life with no meaning, convoluted volition leading to the same result in every endeavor. I could have asked; he wasn't affable for nothing. He'd been around and seemed smart. But too much sensitivity seemed likely. More thinking, more smokes and coffee, a few words, another half laugh and a gaze had become his rote response.

Beyond that, all professorial faculty at the U had committed to the Ph.D.; it was only practical for life in the arts, paradox and irony notwithstanding. Could a person of insight, flourish and articulation striving for beauty forgo rent and groceries? Should art go cold and hungry instead of thriving in reasonable comfort? Could not the Ph.D. provide those things?

I found Ted Moffett at the Hoffbrau House by chance, another in a series of random encounters.

"Oh, fuck no!" he said.

"But ninety-one percent of all National Book Award winners hold the Ph.D."

"Sure, they do! And look what they write! They're boring! Well-written, technically, but do you want to write books like that? Boring books? Books that make people sleepy?"

"Then why do they win?"

"Look at the judges! Ph.Ds.!"

I nodded. Ah, another vicious circle. And he had a greater point. Moreover, truth delivered over a cold beer on a rainy day in a dark bar felt more akin to that reality we held as self-evident.

Ted Moffett was one of us.

We drank and talked. I recalled a Bill Heyden short story he called an old favorite, part of a renowned collection and featured in a magazine. Heyden read it aloud in class, slow enough to trigger a yawn—make that two yawns with the plodding content. A girl goes to a fair and feels dizzy and amazed at the dizzying amazement of reality at the fair; the lights, the colors, the movement. I stayed awake by shaking off the nods, dazed, unamazed.

Ted Moffett said, "No comment."

Bill Heyden gave me a B, mutual reciprocity in our failure to dazzle each other. A grade of B was like an F at that level. Who wants to be a B writer? Who wants to read B novels?

My friend Harold got an A. I reflected on failure in the single area where meaning resided. Harold said that little in academic life had dynamic meaning. "Writing professor," he said. "It's oxymoronic, like passion theory or halting progression."

Yeah. How can an art form get a grade, unless the art is so bad it gets an F? But a B? That's a measure of reader taste. I thought Harold's prose was solid but conventional, conforming to acceptable levels. I said nothing but stewed on Bill Heyden's taste and the potential of second-rate writing.

I thought Bill Heyden academic, his stories analytical and introspective, without action, without spirit, like him. As a classroom kind of guy with affectation, he hadn't mixed it up on the mean streets or high seas, hadn't teased death but looked up at some carnival lights and thought and thought. I thought Ted Moffett correct, more aligned with reality, such as it might be.

With hindsight, I thought I was right; I gave Bill Heyden a C+; counting his affectations for something. But rationalization and glib wit took a while to dull that early sting.

Harold became a dentist. I fell into writing all the time, like a junkie shooting up all the time. I wrote in order to be where I wanted to be. Was that commitment or compulsion? And who gave a fuck? I laughed in the all of it, committed or driven, immersed or submerged, every day, no sweat, happy to be there, high on the flow of it. Writer's block was another laugh, a figment of failed imagination; get the fuck outa here and get outa my way. Short on time and anxious to get things on paper, I stopped, stopped banging my head on the typewriter, stopped moving words from brain to page.

I saw commitment as a forced hand, intellectual, best suited to a Vuhginia drawl. Commitment felt like another spew. Did Bill Heyden talk like that as a child?

I laughed at a punchline. Recalling the old man and Uncle Sammy, lakeside, casting and reeling, beyond commitment, never hoping against hope for a record fish or a mystery fish or a fish that would change fishing. They would have laughed short, lighting new smokes, easing back to contact: a line in the water. The fish was ethereal, caught in the act of fishing.

College was wrong, not just an overwhelming, overbearing waste of time, but dangerous, too. College was for thinking very hard, for mentality, apart and aloof from the world. Writer's block gains currency on campus, because all mind, no body, gets thoughts backed up, constipated.

Music 101 stands alone, an exercise in exception, speaking of irony and paradox. A popular quote of the day was Mahatma Gandhi's response, when asked what he thought of western civilization: "I think it would be a very good idea." To wit: the most advanced nation in world history waged war far away to stop the domino effect of Communism, to control resources and trade. Many people died. The student deferment saved many with course options.

Opting for Music 101, I could get instruction on the instrument of choice. I'd admired Ginger Baker, Ringo, Buddy

Miles and Elvin Jones, thinking many drummers out there just as good without fame. I felt the downbeat but was in for a surprise.

The instructor, a one-off with short hair, plain clothes and a focus on rhythm, taught a snare drum roll. I got it straight away. I'd play gigs in no time. But he said, "That was nice but wrong."

Wrong?

"You're banging the drum."

Yeah? So? I shrugged.

"Don't bang the drum. Lift each beat from the head. Play out of the drum." Playing out of the drum, sum total of the course, required a feel as yet unanticipated. It developed a finer ear, to hear those beats springing from the head instead of driving to the inside.

To this day, "writer's retreat" conjures stillness in a room with a chair, a table, a typewriter and the question, "Now what?" Okay, a computer, but the question remains.

Consideration of the Ph.D. faded fast. And so did college, ending insulation from the hot swamp. I was prime for invitation.

I drew 198 in the draft lottery. Pentagon projection that year went to 195 but depended on body count; if more guys got killed than projected, well then, they'd need more guys to go over. Another summer went down the rathole, waiting for the pre-induction physical required of all males with no exemption. I ditched twenty pounds in thirty days, down to one-seventeen on some Dexedrine Brother scored. He thought they were tens, oops: thirties. Wired in three days instead of three months, I twitched, getting down and dirty, disheveled by design.

I would step apart. All the guys had long hair and pulled the hippie number to fail their physicals. The army doctors got wise in a hurry. Going against the grain, I got skinny as a death-camper and applied what I'd heard or read about, chipping buttons and fingernails, wearing long sleeves and gloves to fade to pale white all over. I got a crew cut to match a rough facial stubble. No tooth brushing or ass wiping, except to scrape some shit residue under chipped fingernails. Strung out, starving, a nervous tick was no act. I was too binged for nuance.

The army doctor said, "Next." But they stopped at 195.

Who said I wasn't stable or sane? I wanted to fail the physical. But the numbers worked out and life began. War is hell and best avoided on a better question. Not *should we fight?* But *will you go?* Each war would generate enough willing fighters or get called off. The Pentagon figured this out, replacing Selective Service with a volunteer army and virtually ending war protest. Volunteers fight for whatever reasons seem acceptable to the general population.

I saw a woman on TV preaching moral imperative for sending US ground troops to the latest region in need. She wore a full-flounced number in flaming red with shoulder pads. But would she have traded for camo fatigues and an M-16? No, not with her importance and agenda.

Year One in the real world went to shitty jobs, dirt labor, shrimp nets, crab pots, digging, heaving, hauling, humping and hating it but doing it. I hit the road for a few thousand miles, got arrested, got out, worked the boats again and finally got a line on

THE ICE KING

a job with a metro daily paper out of Savannah, just up the road from where I'd been shrimping with Jeffrey Baxter.

I'd sold my first story, about Jeffrey, *Edith* and shrimping, to a local monthly for fifty bucks. The editor, big Tim Littleton, said, "I'll tell you what, kid, you got no experience and you're a little bit rough. But goddamn it, you write a mean stick! They don't think twice about this shit, but now they will." He meant those who came down to Hilton Head Island, South Carolina for golf in plaid slacks and white shoes. "They'll love it."

I followed up with another story, a whimsy about variable winds, dreams and island life.

Tim saw my niche, not because I was good but because I wasn't bad. He had very few contributors and liked a writer half his age, casting off for the long crossing. A story a month at fifty bucks a pop was half the rent. I wrote about obvious stuff, wondrous to a new writer who thinks nobody yet wrote about oysters or crabs or lunker bass in tidal creeks or pluff mud or any manner of things good for many months to come. Local color was perfect for a Chamber magazine. Hilton Head Island drew celebrities from the beginning. They came to relax, play golf or have meetings with no media.

Tim Littleton tipped me off one day that the Savannah paper had decided to cover our little island corner of South Carolina. They needed a reporter, not a stringer but a staffer. "I'll tell you the truth, Bobby. I'd be lyin' if I didn't. You don't stand a snowball's chance in hell. Why, every New York newshound'll be on it, once they find out. Cold, miserable bastards. That's what they are. You don't think they'd kill to come down here and live like this? Hell, just relax and have front-page content like what comes in here damn near every day served on a platter? Hell. Not a chance. But I'll tell you what else . . ."

Tim Littleton said he didn't know the Savannah paper well, but he knew it well enough. Editorial staff there would take weeks to process applicants and pick one. Meanwhile, I ought to head on over and say hey. "It ain't but an hour up the road."

I was willing but got stuck on the reality of the situation. "Uh, the thing is, Tim, I . . . never went to J school."

"The hell you say! Why, you coulda stood on your head four years and write a better stick than what they got now! Go get a damn paper and read it, you hear?"

I did and saw straight away that Savannah journalism was who, what, when, where and the facts, no style required or allowed, and no flourish and no irony. *Who the fuck you think you are, bubba? We don't need that shit.* I only imagined that sentiment because it was easy. I'd made slightly less money than rent and groceries for two years, and that felt like a long time. The girlfriend was great, carrying the load, but I'd felt primetime slipping away. It was time to make a move.

Don't misconstrue; that meant it was time for a novel, time for a labor of love with no check on Friday. Time for the saving grace of pure art with talent verging on genius—verging on poverty, too, just add water and saltines.

I'd never made money past basic needs and didn't think I could get the job or make any money to speak of if I did. But another reckoning was upon us. The girlfriend would not say yay or nay but the look said it all, time to break a sweat for money.

What the hell, I'd only be taking a break if the Savannah thing came together, which it likely would not.

Nobody quits art. Art is set aside for practical reasons, pressing needs. Then it fades away, most often. My special coed had put up with an attic apartment, stealing fruit for fun and dinner, menial jobs for chump change from my end of the arrangement. Beyond that, we had artistic delusions and oyster roasts in the backyard.

I said I would not likely get the job.

She shrugged, indifferent to failure but not to effort.

I had the good sense to stay mum.

I called the newspaper that day and asked for the editor.

"What for?"

"The job on Hilton Head Island."

"Who are you?"

"I'm a writer. A reporter."

"Where are you now?"

"I'm here. Hilton Head."

"No. Where you reporting now?"

"I'm here on Hilton Head."

"Hold, please . . ."

The next voice was not so reasonable. "Yenna?" That's old south for hello. We repeated the initial volley, and he said, "Hell, no! You know who I got begging for that job?"

"No."

"Go on down the tennis tournament at the plantation. Gimme color and highlights on the final this afternoon. Six inches. Ten if you need it, but it better be strong."

He hung up.

I called the newsroom for stringer pay.

"It's tin cints a inch."

Okay, I had time. I'd head down to the tennis tournament and knock something out for chump change. Ken Rosewall lost to Aussie star Rod Laver. I didn't care, but it was easy: three column inches on Laver's incredible backhand and seven more on a few highlights. I called the city desk and said I had a story on the Hilton Head tennis. . .

"Read it." I read it, including periods and commas, slow enough for the guy at the other end to knock it out. "Got it."

And that was that. They ran it, no byline. A voice left a message that I'd tallied a dollar on stringer earnings. They'd send a check when I got to five dollars. I was to make sure they had the mailing address.

I called Tim Littleton for more advice on how to go from a dollar to regular pay.

He said, "Aw, hell, just write the damn copy! They got nobody! They got presidential candidates coming in! They got the goddamn governors coming in! Bob Hope for chrissake! Just show up and do the work. They got egg all over their face! They got to take whatever you feed 'em!" In practical education, big Tim had outdistanced a mess o' professors and four years on campus in a minute. "You doin' good, Bobby. Keep it goin'."

"On what? More tennis?"

"No. Hold on."

Tim smoked Salem 100s, claiming they helped curb his appetite. I saw him eat half the Early Bird Breakfast Supreme once, sausage, ham, grits, gravy and three over soft. He left the third egg untouched but not like he didn't want it; he just wanted that Salem 100 more. Life was a bitch for Tim, trying to cut back on what he loved, taking two puffs and sticking the remaining ninety-five millimeters into that yolk. It was disgusting.

Meanwhile, he breathed hard into the phone, scanning his event calendar. "Well, no tennis or golf for a few weeks. Hell, call the sheriff over in Bluffton. About seven a.m. Now listen here: you tell them you calling for the crime report. You with the Savannah paper. You gonna get rape and murder damn near any morning you want. That's bread and butter for a metro daily, you hear? You nobody. They don't need you. But you here! They need the dateline! That's Hilton Head Island, SC, and you the only goddamn person alive to give it."

"Yes, sir."

Day 2 started on a rape/homicide in a trailer park halfway up to Beaufort. "Uh . . . emeesee here, accidents. Okay, they's a head-on crash out to Savannah highway, one dead, two critical. No names, pending notification to next o' kin."

I knocked it out and called it in, only seven inches but what the hell.

The voice on the other end said to call twenty minutes earlier tomorrow instead of slamming their asses up against deadline like a know-nothing cub idiot.

I did that, too, and added a second story when a huge yacht came in and another when Spiro T. Agnew, Vice President of the United States of America, arrived in a helicopter on the eighteenth fairway for a very important meeting with some very important men.

Talk about simpler times; I strolled the rotor radius to ask, "Why are you here, Mr. Vice President?" The throwaway question revealed me: green and toothless. He looked me up and down and walked away. He could have tossed a bone to the second biggest metro daily in a major southern state. What could a few words cost? *Boy, you got a beautiful place here.* But no. He opted for no warmth, no risk, nothing quotable and no intention but to keep the pup hungry.

Spiro T. Agnew got caught stealing huge money and would have gone to prison but for *nolo contendere—I'll admit it if I don't have to do the time.* Then he died.

I got skunked on Spiro T., but hardly an hour later, Roger Mudd showed up from *CBS News* on another helicopter, down the same fairway, fairly ending the media-free zone that had been Hilton Head Island. I strolled along with him, too, and asked, "Why are you here, Roger?"

He kept walking, sizing me up, and said, "The vice president of the United States is meeting in private with the governor of South Carolina to talk about revenue sharing." He stopped and turned. "There's your story. They both want it but still need to figure out how to get it." Roger Mudd had read me quick, green and in need. He fed the pup.

I made the front page of Section B on a four-inch thumbnail and remember Roger Mudd as a generous man. Moreover, I learned the next day that the Southern Governor's Conference would convene at the Hilton Head Inn in two weeks. I drove to

Savannah and walked into Wally Davis's office, unannounced. We'd spoken on the phone, but he asked, "Who you?"

"I'm your Hilton Head man. I'm all over the Southern Governor's Conference. As staff, Hilton Head Island Correspondent. No more stringer stuff."

"No way in hell! You know who I got begging for that spot? Why, I . . ."

"I'm there. I got a place with a desk and a telephone. I got a fridge and a bed, too. Conference in two weeks. All the southern governors. All the media, except for you."

"You'll be there."

"I'll be there if you want me to be there."

We danced our minuet through job requirements, including the crime report every morning for the evening press and nonstop celebrity coverage for the morning news. "That's two or three stories every day and a Sunday feature once a month. And it better be good. A hundred forty dollars a week and not one damn cent more . . ."

HA! LELUJAH!

HA! LELUJAH!

HALELUJAH! HALELUJAH!

Dumbfounded, I could only nod and head out.

"Hey!" Wally called.

I turned back.

"You got a college degree?"

"Yeah." And I did, hanging over Mother's TV, lone remnant of the four-year alternative to the jungle war.

Wally didn't ask for that detail, but I'd have said as much if he had. As it was, I was happy to use that degree and happier still, knowing I didn't need it.

I'd written more in a short stint as stringer for the Savannah papers than in four years of college. I doubt that Managing Editor Wally Davis gave a flat flying fuck about a college degree but had rules to follow. He likely wondered what took me so long to put paper in my Smith Corona and knock it out. Then again, things had moved right along, given limitations and adaptations.

Newspaper work cuts a writer's teeth. The college degree required eight short stories in four years, but the sensitive stuff goes south in a heartbeat on a metro daily. Forget ambiance and mood, inspiration and feelings; knock it out. The sheriff's report—rapes and murders, death and dismemberment—helped the caffeine kick in and fingers fly across the keys. Brutality and ignorance are novelties at first but sink in fast, no joke.

Two or three hard news stories every day needed coverage, writing and transmission by three. On a slow news day, an assignment came over, something soft, like a flower show, a handicapped kid at the beach, the new chair of a women's club, all soft. I had a Sunday feature on a subject of my choosing once a month, also soft. "And make it inoffensive and noncontroversial, goddamn it!"

Those days made for skill in honing to the crux on the first go. Mornings opened on coffee, rape and murder. Restraint, silence, goodwill and healing sentiment were out the window, roadside rubbish, yesterday's paper. Domestic brutality fed the volunteer army. "Well sir, we got us a grand theft auto, assault with a DWI and two . . . no, three rapes . . . hell, I can't tell if it was three bucks on a gangrape or one buck on three rapes. Hold on, Bub, I be right back atcha."

The critically maimed required follow up, so I called the hospital, too, because the public has a right to know.

I hated it when no celebrities came to town. They were fun and easy news. Without them, we fell back on rape, murder, recipes, gardening and endless resort development.

Finally, two weeks onto the payroll, the Southern Governor's Conference came to town in a dog 'n pony to remember, every gov glowing in the darkness of political pursuit, primed for greatness. All the southern governors and a few strays had joined the presidential scrum. All three networks (1972: CBS, NBC, ABC) and journalistic all-stars converged on my beat.

Huge sliding doors got pulled back on three banquet rooms to make a pressroom for the working press. That phrase often compensates for low self-esteem, stipulating that it's a job, not a cakewalk. What else can they call it? The drinking press? The aggressive press?

About a hundred small desks with typewriters filled the pressroom, with telephones nearby, along with paper, pens, the works. Talk about high tech; the back wall had banquet tables end-to-end with a few dozen Telecopiers, unbelievable gizmos that could grab a page of copy on a platen and roll it past an optic eye for transmission to anywhere in four minutes!

Once uptown, ain't no goin' back to the farm. I requested and got my own Telecopier hardly a month in, no more reading comma, clarifying comma or repeating as necessary period.

But that was later. The pressroom got crowded as the set-ups went into place, all these guys banging away, and I thought, *What? It hasn't even started.* They looked focused and purposeful. I sat down, fed a sheet and typed. I wanted to make a go of it. I wanted to fit in.

Dear Mother,

The guy next to me looks tired and alcoholic. I think he's trying to see my work. I've been so hungry lately . . .

My newspaper career resides in a loose-leaf binder beside the college stories. All sat in Brother's dining room hutch. My newsroom letter to Mother is page one in the binder.

She'd asked for months, "Is this it? I mean this thing that you do. What do you call it? Writing?"

I didn't call it writing, and I was getting paid. I got lunch with the local shirts at the Rotary club on Wednesdays in trade for covering their guest speaker. I interviewed celebrities in a steady stream. She seemed slightly appeased at that. I did not say that it wouldn't last, that it wasn't what I longed for, which was real writing, fiction writing, with breaking waves, secret caves, hidden treasure and the lore of lost youth. I stayed with what passed for journalism for the learning curve and the money. Monthly magazine stories made for mad money. I did not explain these things to Mother but said, "Yes. It's what I do. You can call it what you want. Writing, journalism, anything."

She didn't moan or tsk, tsk, but I could hear her head shaking; she could not call it the law or medicine.

I went back to the Telecopiers, making a show of it, as if Mother had one and could receive. She didn't, and at the far end of that table, I folded the letter in thirds and half again for a back pocket. Heading out to the lobby, I wondered what next, along with who, when and where.

A small entourage and a feeble old man came on, recognizable a few paces out. Lawrence E. Spivak, journalistic icon and pioneer in TV news founded *Meet the Press* in '45 and hosted for twenty-eight years, predating Walter Cronkite. I'd watched, riveted on core intellect so sharp it felt like action.

I stopped.

Lawrence Spivak smiled.

"Hello, Mr. Spivak."

"Hello to you, sir," he nodded, moving on.

I didn't care about celebrity but tingled in his wake.

Coffee, tea and water stations lined the lobby among plush chairs and couches. I got a coffee and sat, briefly, because the working press doesn't rest for long. I opened my notebook to jot a few notes but had only Revenue Sharing. It was the hot topic and would dominate the conference. Many people rambled rhetorically but made no sense—not to me. Revenue is money coming in. Sharing is giving part of what you have to others. I didn't get it and didn't know who to ask. Revenue Sharing was Dick Nixon's baby. It was an election year, and the Solid South, all Democratic, would be crucial to passage. I could fathom no meaning or importance or drama. The revenue was gone to federal coffers, to be stolen, squandered or fractionally spent for the betterment of all. So? What was new? That Dick Nixon would let state governments into the cookie jar?

Unfazed, I would try a few moves I'd seen in others, or so I thought. Another small entourage entered the lobby, this time surrounding a medium fat man who stopped to assess the room. Many years later, Terminator would scan like that, calibrating threat potential on advanced telemetry. South Carolina Governor John West was a politico, entrenched in practicality. Non-dynamic and bland, he lit up like a dim bulb and proceeded, detecting no threat or potential.

I waited with a question and a reporter's notebook.

He stopped, a gamesman move.

I stepped up. "Governor West," I began.

"Who are you with?" he asked.

"*Savannah Morning News & Evening Press.*"

He smiled on a head tilt. The second biggest newspaper in Georgia was not the local tabloid, but it wasn't a South Carolina paper either. The Savanna paper had a South Carolina edition but with infinitesimal readership next to the Columbia paper. John West asked, "What's your question?"

"What do you think of revenue sharing?" I'd tipped my hand and showed nothing. What an empty question.

He replied in kind with a soft harrumph and strolled on. Two of his crew glanced my way with soft scorn of their own.

I thought John West an asshole, best at self-aggrandizement. But the news depends on assholes, and I'd failed. I sat back down to my coffee, cooled. I thought to refresh it but didn't know why or much else. I thought to build a story around a comment from a neighboring governor but doubted I'd get next to Georgia Gov Jimmy Carter, an up-and-comer with a huge grin, a peanut farmer, new on the political scene and seen as formidable, what with his smarts and honesty. Moreover, his entourage was thicker 'n yesterday's gravy, staffers and news dogs clamoring after the Georgia phenom with the teeth.

I had to check my program to see that Robert Scott was governor of North Carolina, which felt lukewarm on political dynamics. His photo looked generic, forgettable in a blink. Still, I looked at it for a match with any man entering the lobby, entourage not required. Come on. North Carolina?

I roamed back down the corridor, in and out of the pressroom, into a meeting that was open to the working press, back to the lobby and home for a sandwich and a lie down. I hated feeling so damn uncertain. Deadline for the *Evening News* was two p.m. It came and went. The city desk called after four, closer to five. "Whaddaya got?"

"Revenue Sharing."

"What's the lead?"

"Revenue Sharing."

"What about it? You got an angle?"

"I'm working on it."

"When?"

"It won't be long now."

I reported to the city editor, who ran the desk by the book.

He hung up. He sounded peeved, normal for him.

I headed back down to the conference, wondering what, who and the rest. I mingled, late in the day, the entourages and politicos having mostly retreated to their bunkers as I had done, though they hosted strategy sessions, with cocktails. Remaining persons seemed nondescript, and I did not see North Carolina Governor Who's It. Mundane as he seemed, I was ready to seek his thoughts on Revenue Sharing. He seemed good for a quote instead of a half-smile, but he didn't show.

I went to the bar for a beer. I had nothing and solid prospects for more. I had another beer. Resort hotel drinking was extravagant, but the tough day had taken a greater toll.

Dusk faded to twilight, and I walked out to nightfall.

Standing out front of the Hilton Head Inn, wondering what to do with so much nothing, I looked left and right, as if for an arrival. I waited but couldn't say what for, and a limo pulled up.

Two security guys came out, not hotel security but guys in black suits, heavies. They looked me over.

I stepped aside.

Jimmy Carter and wife Rosalynn came out jabbering, and she grasped his arm for the two steps down.

A security guy jogged to the limo to open the door.

They moved to it but stopped, seeing me on the sideline, watching, notebook in hand and, I suppose, forlorn in the face. I don't know that she gave his arm another squeeze, but I thought she did. Jimmy turned my way, stepping up, offering his hand. "Hi. I'm Jimmy Carter."

I blushed and shook it.

"Get your story?"

I shook my head, stupefied and tongue-tied.

"You local?"

I shook again and said, "Savannah. *Morning News & Evening Press*." Jimmy and Roz shared another blip, knowing full well the power of the second biggest metro daily in Georgia, behind the *Atlanta Constitution.*

He sat down on the edge of a masonry planter and patted the space beside him. Sure, it was a setup on a shoo-in, a good one.

Roz slid in on my other side, leaning in to listen.

I opened my notebook.

Jimmy asked, "What is Revenue Sharing?"

I looked up, so he could see my eyes roll.

He laughed. "Okay. It's simple . . ."

It wasn't simple. It was dull. But I took notes.

Roz leaned in. "You know, Jimmy is the only govnah here who doesn't like it."

She'd fed me the lead.

Jimmy said, "I'm the only governor here at this conference who is opposed to Revenue Sharing. Let me tell you why." And he did, slowly, so I could keep up, taking it down. He managed the situation, a young cub in need of feeding, and a seasoned candidate of wit and wisdom, taking time for that feeding, for the betterment of all.

The limo waited, motor running, security guys scanning.

In a few minutes, he stood.

Roz and I stood.

"Thank you, son. What's your name?"

I said, "No. Thank *you*," and told him my name.

Roz leaned in again, "We'll look for your story. I know it'll be good." She rubbed a hand across my shoulders.

Jimmy offered another shake. I took it. He put his free hand on our clasp, infusing the power unto him and me. He beamed, and they left, he and Roz, the security team and entourage.

In the next week I would ask to be bureau chief.

Wally Davis would smolder and curse, until I told him I needed no Indians and no more pay, explaining the benefits of a stronger title for a vital correspondent.

He grumbled but didn't say no. And so it came to pass.

Meanwhile, I hit the pressroom, empty but for stragglers, know-nothings most likely, knocking out letters to their mothers. I knocked out thirty column-inches, reread for typos and clarity and marched it over to the Telecopier. Twenty minutes later, I called the city desk.

Joe answered, seven p.m., five hours past deadline, three hours past drop-deadline.

I asked, "You get it?"

"Hold on." He shuffled pages and took a minute. "Good stuff. Okay, ask him if . . ."

"He's gone."

"Gone?"

"With the wind."

"Okay. Good stuff. Very good stuff. I'm gonna bump John West from the South Carolina side and run this up front, all editions. Strong, solid stuff. Hey. We got a picture a you?"

He meant front page, at the top. I went home, had another beer and went to whiskey, to commemorate passage from one thing to another.

The magazine office was a regular visit, dropping off stories, picking up checks, hanging out, chewing the fat with Tim or the crew. I felt kinship and good intentions.

Linda the receptionist greeted with a pretty face and warm manner, attentive and taking in stride the eyeballs of men settling to her chest. I imagined her rationale: *well, heck, they just men, doin' what they do.*

Likable and sweet, Linda had a lumpy husband who defied accountability on taste in women. Or in Linda's taste at any rate; she could have done better.

He got home shortly before she did and waited.

She got home and submitted to his hand up her dress, daily.

Not a foreplay kind of guy, he'd maneuver, pull it out and sniff it for sperm. He knew his wife was weak, and every man wanted her. Why wouldn't they? And he wasn't about to do nothing while she buried the big salami.

This info came from Ruth, office secretary, who seemed distressed to the point of sharing.

We talked when I came in with stories or had to wait to see big Tim. We talked about the new shopping strip, comings and goings, small talk, dull and predictable. Linda took care on delivery of stories and checks, and when the talk went domestic, she seemed in need of a sympathetic ear, maybe distressed like Ruth. I didn't mind. She said she read my stories and thought I was the best writer around, one of the best she'd read. She made me weak with understanding.

She told about hubby and finger check.

I got a hot flash. Why would she lead me into that maze? I loved experience, the stuff of great stories, but this seemed strange and tricky.

For better or worse, I came around late. Tim and Ruth left at three but the office stayed open to five, so it was just Linda and me. Open, abused, perceptive and stacked, she lit up.

It seemed like an unusual chat between friends, and that was a good thing. We could talk, her married, me with a girlfriend. But in very short order, as men do, I wanted Linda like I wanted New York.

Hubby was right.

I imagined a story, clever gothic, where the outside guy leaves a slug o' maple syrup down there, and Hubby asks, *What in a hell? Why, Issiz maple syrup!* Or, in Carolina parlance, *maypull surp*. I thought maple syrup would be a nice twist, good for a laugh.

I told her I was on my way to the post office and needed a manila envelope, if she had one.

"You bet," she said, heading to the supply room that had no windows, one door.

I followed, as if to share the load. In the supply room, she bent over. I steadied and stepped up but chickened out.

She stood and turned with an envelope and a blush. "You cain't make a omelet," she said, closing the distance.

We embraced. We kissed, trembling. I released her buttons and the big hooks that held the harness in place.

She's only human, I thought, *lonely, confused and dreamy*. I freed her from bondage and gazed, dumbfounded, as she knelt to my bondage and proceeded to more freedom. Though gratifying in the physical sense, she talked through it, hating that bastard.

In the aftermath, when men think about dinner and the game, she said. "I'm glad we did that. I really wanted you to have it. God, if he ever found out."

"What would he do?"

"He wouldn't do nothing to me. He'd kill you. He's insane. I don't even care. I want to do it again, all the time."

"Yes. Again. Sometime. You have to be home soon."

"I can't wait." She seemed cheerful, rejuvenated. "I'm gonna breathe on him."

Oh, God.

"I'm gonna tell him I had gator tail for lunch."

I'd thought her sweet and simple, a victim of circumstance.

That was '73 or '74. Females today seem less likely to put up with pussy check, but you never know. The maple syrup story dribbled and faded, stranger than fiction.

I quit newspaper work and writing for the local magazine a year later when a sportfishing tournament came to the island. I would learn in very few years to loathe that action; big, fat men killing noble beasts for photo ops and dumping the corpses.

At the time, I pursued color and action. Joe said no, not for a regular story or a Sunday feature. I argued but lost and went anyway. I sold the story to a New York magazine for five hundred dollars on the first try. Five hundred was ten months of local magazine writing, more than three weeks of newspaper work, but that was my last week. I had other bones to pick.

At age twenty-four, I thought of it as five hundred bucks for a day's work, and five or ten such days each month would mean bigger money at a higher level. I thought things were playing out, and the real writing life had begun. Sadly, I was correct on the reality part but not so much on the return.

The next eighteen months were bleak. A dozen more scores in New York felt like good work for good pay, but those twelve scores took about six weeks each, ass kissing, preselling and scrambling all the way. And for what? Five bills each? I'd be better off writing a novel, I thought.

Bleak got worse. The former girlfriend had become the wife and split. Who could blame her, in her prime, hooked up with a dreamer? The bond had softened, those formative years forming different people, more or less, than the kids we'd been.

She remained nice.

I'd turned to irony, dark humor and pathos, too skewed for polite company. I never thought regular work was for losers or nondreamers who threw in the towel, only that it wasn't for me.

She felt the skew, seeing a guy with his head in the sand and the clouds, a guy disconnected from rent, groceries and other fundamentals, a guy who didn't fit, often by choice, a guy who stayed broke by choice with one prospect, a million-to-one shot, on the nose: *Once upon a time . . .*

I didn't blame her, but then I did.

She knew risk/reward on blind faith and art, or said she did. She lost patience. She wanted a return in a timely manner. She saw guys who'd made it, guys with new cars, real jobs and income, guys who came on to her even though she was married, like the guys Linda's husband worried about.

I'd planned to make her happy, once truth and beauty paid out, when narrative flourish flowed with revenue.

Two years in and counting, she made other plans, taking Margaret Mead's advice, that life comes in parts, each with a fortune and a husband. I thought that convenient and shallow. We drifted apart to pursue our disparate dreams. John Lennon said, "Life is long." Done with the sunny southland, its limitations, fat people and failure to imagine, she went.

I let her go, sensing better work without the distraction of her mundane appetites and needs. So began my next chapter: *Still Life in Winter*. Talk about better conditions for artistry; it got down to eight bucks on a gray day in February, frosty dawn to dusk going dark along with prospects. No fuel in the furnace or food on the table, payments late, sick with flu. Both cats under the covers, hungry, meowed the question of the hour: who would die first, them or me?

The novel was coming along.

Anyone could solicit an agent in the mid-'70s, but to call a publisher directly, to speak with a goddess of the industry, took a reference. I finished my novel and made many calls, sent many copies, took shitty jobs, starved and drank like Ted Moffett and the old man. It went on for months.

Down to seeds and stems, empty cupboard and fridge, necessity became another mother. I went to see a guy, new in town, down for a project and dating a woman I knew. I thought I could borrow fifteen grand to leverage a small building, say four apartments, and convert to condominiums and sell. Condo conversion was his specialty, and the South was ripe for a profit phenom. I told him I was good, a natural who needed front-end guidance.

He talked me through it and said, "I've combed the place. I don't think you'll find anything. But if you find something outa your range, let me know." He could go a million. With million-dollar range in 1979, who needed to stay poor?

I found it. We did it. I made forty grand on another growth curve. I couldn't retire but felt wealthy. I pondered a new book in the new current that flowed more freely.

A letter came from New York, not a form rejection but personal. A literary agent saw merit in my manuscript and a potential career in fiction. I scanned for the kill, for the *unfortunately, you sorry chump, we can't* . . . for the farewell and best of luck in placing your manuscript elsewhere. But it only said yes.

And they're off! Yahoo!

Barbara Nance, also formative, would spend three years pounding Manhattan pavement, talking and lunching with editors. Each meeting ended on the same bullshit spew of greatness, fabulous and fantastic, but alas. It wasn't right for their lists. They wouldn't know how to sell it. A list is focused on a market segment, a niche. Calling a book great but not right for a list is like saying, *You know I love you, I really do. But I don't.*

How did control of literature get so centralized, like in the Soviet Union? The literary market reflected academia, not society. The advanced degree was currency. The academic complex ruled. Narrative voices achieved sameness, expressing social mores in boilerplate and cliché. Men softened. Women pummeled. Women demanded. Women needed. It was high time, with specific regard to love, divorce and feelings in New York.

Not fitting a list got paradoxical. List-fit felt prearranged on connections in the social matrix known as market demand. Some shitty books sold better than other shitty books, and better sales led to more shitty books of similar nature. The system generated sequels and look-alikes.

I paraphrased for my agent. "Lists show who's kissing ass according to form."

She asked, "Is that nice? Or necessary?"

I replied, "No. It's not nice. I can't tell what's necessary."

"I can. Why don't you forget about this? Let me worry. You should be starting something new."

Barbara Nance understood. With her on point, I didn't offend anyone in New York. I ranted in a padded cell. She said I reminded her of Scott Fitzgerald. She calmed me.

She peddled it, visiting some publishers two and three times, because editors turn over. She'd call again for a better fit on a new list at a new place with an old editor, or the old place with a new editor. She worked it, reporting literary accolade.

In a year, Barbara quit the big agency to hang her own shingle. I could stay with the big agency, under contract with a new agent; she didn't know who. Or I could roll the bones with her. That would make her happy, she said. Her new agency would be nonfiction with one exception, an author who could tell a story like Scott Fitzgerald and write it better.

Shit, I thought. She thinks I'm better than I think I am. That perception and faith are uncommon, hitherto only in Mother. I took three hours to call back, to say yes, again yes.

She'd moved to her own office. I asked for the number.

The voice at the old agency asked, "Who are you? Are you a client? Does she know you? Are you fiction?"

"Yes, I'm fiction."

Conventional approach had proved impractical to me and my father before me. I'd been delusional and failed. Faith seemed a ruse, untrue, until Barbara Nance. Racing forms were for bettors who didn't know Mr. Billberry. Barbara said we would win.

I called the new number. Barbara answered, a warm voice in New York.

In six-month intervals we had deals at St. Martins, where it died in Paperback; at Elizabeth Von Schnitt, who vanished into thin air; with Margaret Snowdon, who'd been doing much better at her new job but relapsed and went away. On again, off again, we churned to butter like the tiger's tail.

"Don't think that," Barbara said. "It's no different on any book. I'll worry about it. Not you. Start another book."

Three years of it led to a dozen new synopses for editors who wanted to see a different slant here or there. I accepted the harness and pulled, repressing thoughts of a marriage failed, insolvency and waste. In the days of no computers, a clean page got typed in full with minimal Wite-Out.

IBM came forth like a NASA moon shot with Selectric II and a button to back the typing ball and strike the error. Life did not improve but took less time.

Better still, Barbara called. "Okay, Bobby. We're on."

I'd heard it before. I was stoned, which was better than drunk, less damaging, more healthful. "But are we high?"

"Are you doubting me?"

"No!"

"Okay, look. I can't talk now. I didn't tell you about this one because, well, you know."

"I know."

"She read it. She loves it. She's young and red hot. She's scored on every list so far and anything she touches is a go."

That meant the manuscripts this editor had chosen for development and publication on her employer's lists had made money. Her employer was Seaview Books. "It's the hardcover, literary arm of Playboy Books." The hot young editor used to be elsewhere and was on a roll.

But arrival held back. Numbing, doubtful, it recalled the old man's loan approval to save the oil wells. Eyes opened, his and mine, on hearing yes, the dream would happen. Wouldn't it?

Barbara couldn't talk. She'd stopped down on the street at a payphone to call with the news. We said goodbye.

I didn't believe it for three days, until she called again and spoke of our deal as solid. I believed. We were on, sucked through the black hole of acceptance in New York.

"Should I come?"

"I don't think so. Don't worry about that. You're going to be very busy on rewrites, new angles, all that."

"I love rewrites, new angles, all that."

"Hey. Congratulations. I'll generate two-hundred-fifty thousand dollars this year. Your book counts for less than one percent, and I think you're my hottest property."

Well, shut my mouth.

"I'll call you," she said. She would forward directly all Sheila's preliminary notes. We would review. Sheila was the red-hot young editor.

I flew to New York the following week to feel fame and money in the making. I felt stuck in South Carolina, done with cracker barrel, shoo-fly, antebellum nonsense anyway. Easy socially, the place had a limited view, no new thinking, no nothing but high tide, low tide, Scotch and history. Everything felt pickled as a pig foot in a jar. Rightwing Christians sprouted like spore growth.

I would move to San Francisco at last, after visiting New York.

I checked into the Chelsea Hotel and met Barbara for dinner after three years of letters and phone. Physical presence was good. I was nearly thirty. She was twenty-eight but older, city smart and business smart, a seasoned New Yorker, a mover and a closer. Nicer than I was but tougher, she showed panache and instinct. Fast friends in a few minutes, we set business aside for personal stuff over dinner and wine.

I told stories. She loved listening to a country mouse recall a few big cats.

She loosened up, into the wine, feeling the rarest commodities in The Apple: friendship and trust. Her name wasn't always Barbara Nance, nor had she been the person sitting before me. "Rhoda Gershenstein. How far can you get on a name like that?" She laughed at the Rhoda Gershenstein Agency.

"I think you'd be as far along by any name."

"Barbara Nance is strong. I wanted away from Rhoda Gershenstein. Her life was sad." She smiled sadly.

I poured more wine for stories of the city.

As a child, chained to the radiator, her stepfather diddled, tweaked, burned and raped her fifteen years before child abuse became a media phenom, a hub of self-discovery. She made my past look like the teddy bears' picnic.

I poured to douse discomfort. She drank and went on, sharing with a friend.

She felt restored when the bastard died. Her mother committed suicide soon after, when Rhoda was a teen, a year before her big-hearted brother got drafted to Viet Nam, to step off the plane into shrapnel. Rhoda changed to Barbara, a refresh. She sipped. "Sorry."

I took her hand. "Thank you for being you."

We savored our union.

Boyish adventures seemed long ago, casual and carefree. Her past cleaved the air to a Grand Canyon of vulnerability. I'd been roughed up; she'd been brutalized. Our three-year campaign had marinated on wine and the carnage before us.

She choked up, saying she didn't share her background in town but thought I should know. She hoped we'd stay together.

I took her other hand. "Nobody else but my mother has faith in me. I'll treasure you, no matter what."

Too sentimental for comfort, we shared pain and potential. Her confidence felt monumental. I felt lucky. I loved what she'd given, but . . . It felt wobbly.

We said goodnight with a hug. She'd cried at dinner and cried again, saying I was the most terrific writer alive today.

I wanted to believe but learned early to dismiss praise along with the other. We had baggage. Well, who doesn't? She excelled as an agent. I would know her forever, starting the next day, when we'd try to close a deal.

We met for the hallowed ritual: lunch. The cheesy little deli served cheese sandwiches on paper plates and sodas in bottles, making the stodgy South look all the more pleasant. Never mind. Who could eat, with greatness on the table?

Barbara had firmed up, back to business.

Sheila wore an icy glare and keen edge. Consensus was that literature and history were in the making. Sheila was a great young editor on the scene with Barbara, the miracle agent of the season, a quarter-mil in contracts annual. As the sizzling secret, the writer who would not wait for a third or fifth novel to emerge, I would break out on novel one. We imagined headlines, as people in New York do. "I'm thinking front page," Sheila said, meaning the *New York Times Book Review*.

"Oh, yes," Barbara said. "I'm not even worried about that. The important thing is, this will be your breakout."

Like a bumpkin, I soaked it up. New Yorkers love bumpkins, soft spoken and toothless. I felt the love. Greatness filled in, rearranging a writer's life.

Everything needed rewriting, re-angling, before Sheila could structure the deal, but don't worry; the deal was foregone.

I flew home wondering why I'd gone to New York, questioning stability, fearing the phantom in every corner, every voice and volition in The Apple. Barbara and I needed each other. Why would she open her soul to someone flying out in hours? Well, that seemed why, and who could blame her in a nutty place like that?

I drove to California in an ancient Ford Falcon wagon, battered but not beat. We'd get by on wrenches, a ratchet and sockets, reefer, cooler, typewriter and bedding. I'd forwarded mail to an old sailing friend's house in California, and a Christmas card from Barbara waited my arrival. She wished for joy, now and always.

A week later, Sheila called, sobbing. Barbara had taken her own life. "It was so awful," Sheila gasped. Barbara overdosed on Christmas Eve, after telling everyone she was off to the Hamptons "for holiday."

I'd migrated to life as an author in California. I'd set up a card table and a chair at my friend's place, planning to look for my own place in a day or two. An author gets to work, deferring mundane chores to spare time.

The haymaker was a roundhouse right to the nose. Impact came in waves. Numbness stunned like the end of the world. I replayed, as people do. Had I been remiss in failing to see Barbara's need?

Sheila ditched the quiver to talk business. She'd quit as red-hot editor. It was this thing with Barbara. It was time, her time. It had come and could wait no longer. She would write, to answer her own call of greatness.

Greatness was again presumed, but she seemed clear, likely with a connection in mind. She knew the ins and outs and could finagle an obscene advance and hyped promo as well as the next aspirant. Her book would be great, she said.

I felt slammed, a nobody like everybody, as it would be.

Sheila said to call anytime in the next week. She'd be wrapping up. Then she'd be "out of pocket."

I moved five times in the next year, scaling down, spending a thousand hours on long talks to New York and a thousand more in rewriting, re-angling, reconsidering perspectives for a dozen New Yorkers who knew of Barbara's faith and what must be right in me. All faded directly.

I think few people can prevent a suicide. Barbara would have likely fared best with a friend from afar. Should I have stayed longer or visited again or called? I couldn't know.

For money, I wrote promotional brochures for an investment real estate company: rent caps, upside potential, depreciation, tax credits and worse. And I joined the army after all, the San Francisco army of waiters, waitresses, copy writers, maids, cab drivers, bellhops, you-name-its, foot soldiers of failure in the arts, the frontline faithful, blind to the reality of day in, day out.

It came to nothing and worse: poverty and burnout. I asked the people of publishing, please, run me around the block. They complied. The continuing New York consensus: not quite right for the list, any list.

By '83, I estimated that I'd written or rewritten ten thousand pages in ten years and gave it up. I sailed to Hawaii on a hot yacht, bought on dummied tax returns and faux pro forma to guaranty success on the far shore in a fool's paradise.

I'd knock out thirty thousand more pages in the next ten years, until they read like a mantra, piss and vinegar achieving ultimate numbness on no impact. It felt like the beating some people need, to wise up.

Luck factored, too; Mr. Billberry failed to show.

People visiting the tropics like to watch fish while sucking air through a plastic tube. A pursuit finally paid, didn't hurt anyone and nobody got pissed. It was simple, if only a kid could get out of the way, showcase an attitude, let them laugh in contact with others more colorful and graceful than themselves.

It worked, no pro forma, loan ap or finagling, just supply to meet demand, like the old country magic from far away, long ago. Success hinged on magic stored from youth. The basics were honesty and humor with a few punch lines.

For years, big seas and haunted houses gave me the willies. I wondered if I'd go for a million bucks and thought yes, I'd set fear aside to change life forever. Life changes anyway. Money is everything, if you don't have it. With money, old fears can feel nostalgic. Comfort gets boring. I accepted failure and made money. When the time came, it felt like a walk in the park.

Mother said that I sought to be somewhere else from early childhood, off to a different story. Along the way, across continents, oceans and years, I lost the manuscript I'd followed to New York. I thought such losses neither accidental nor bad. The manuscript took years, all lost. It was a Jonah; best forgotten, I thought. Searching every box, shelf or odd space at odd intervals, I knew it had to be somewhere. It wasn't, but I found a few rejections and a rewrite of the first hundred twenty-five pages.

Well, it wasn't that good, overwritten, oddly structured with a few decent passages. I scanned the rewrite; rhapsodic, descriptive, too much. One rejection said, *You are a fine writer indeed, and rereading your manuscript reminds me how much I love the parts that I love. I just don't feel confident that our list could* blah, blah, blah . . .

I wondered if red-hot Sheila had given Barbara the nod because red-hotness can cool in a blink, and Sheila was worried, and Barbara was coming on. Ah, who knows?

Having rent and groceries covered soothed the pain, eased regrets and resentment. Potential can fool anybody, with people talking greatness as others poo-pooed and would again. Who do you believe, if luck takes a holiday?

Greatness in a story needs time to emerge, to outlive commercial trends. I never stopped writing through thick and thin, in sickness and in health. I wrote to Bill Heyden for guidance on my commitment. He didn't answer.

In '92, I called the big agency in New York where Barbara Nance worked in '76. Did they know Sheila, the red-hot editor? A woman said, "I know of her. One of her clients just quit her, to come to me, for better service."

I got Sheila's new number and called. She became a literary agent when she gave up writing, greatness being so elusive and unwieldy. A fellow in Sheila's office asked, "Who are you? Are you a client?"

"It's a long story," I said.

"She's extremely busy. She can't just talk. Besides, she's on another line. Hold on." I held. "She's talking to California!"

I said I needed help in finding someone who'd known Barbara, who might know where to find the old manuscripts.

"Twelve years? Impossible!"

"At least remote," I said. "I'd like to ask Sheila."

"Hold on." A few minutes later, he said, "I'm sure she doesn't know."

"Can I speak with her?"

"She's too busy. She might be busy ten minutes!"

"I'll hold."

I held.

"Look. She doesn't know, okay? She says she was never friends with Barbara Nance. Okay?"

"Okay."

"Have a nice day," the fellow said.

I let go again, let go of hope that anyone in New York heard anything but the distant echo of greatness. I heard it, sitting at Brother's dining room table that morning in '92, hardly a month after the nervous fellow in red-hot Sheila's office assured that all was lost . . . and BOOM! I saw it, the one place that long lost manuscript could be: in the dusty stack on Brother's hutch.

I put two phone books on a chair and reached yet again.

Brother made new coffee and pursued his morning routine.

I'd arrived fifteen hours prior but long ago. I tossed old papers onto the table, looking, retrieving.

Another Saturday at Brother's was officially underway on cartoons with space monsters and a starlet with huge breasts and quivering lips, both idiotic. Next up: *The Smurfs.*

Outside, Lucy and Ethel had finished pissing and whined to get in from the cold. "How can you watch that shit?"

Brother shushed, stoked his bong and said, "It's Saturday."

He came to the dining room, pissed off at the mess I made.

I told him I needed an old manuscript.

He said, "It's not there."

I let it go once more, dressed and went for a walk, for distance from Brother's kaleidoscope. I needed air. It felt like cold steel on the inhale A walk around the block was painful. I considered pain and thought stinging cold the worst.

I considered justice and thirty years. How much of life is lost, waiting? I supposed that's where other interests were meant to take over, or at least distract. But had spiritual dysfunction stuck me in a wallow? My corner man still urged a pop in the nose. But to what benefit? Could I let go of anything?

Thoughts and snowflakes drifted around Brother's block. I got back as Mother and Sissy arrived. It felt like the future, a Saturday morning with the family as different from thirty years ago as the Midwest is different from the tropics.

But maybe not; Brother watched cartoons. Mother cooked. Sissy was on the phone, and I was happily free of school.

Inside, once the dogs stopped yapping and the coats got hung, and Brother told everyone to shut the fuck up so he could hear the cartoons, and Mother spoke the menu, and Sissy said she didn't have time, we reached a lull.

It was brief.

"I don't want to dwell on the morbid," Mother said. "But I'm meeting with the rabbi to talk about a plot. They're not easy to get anymore, and I need to know how many, I mean, together."

Presenting eternity on a Saturday morning from the kitchen, on a casual approach to the bones, she asked in the same minute how many bagels and how many graves. She looked my way, hopeful for a homecoming at last.

"I'm comfortable in the tropics for now," I said.

"Okay" she said, turning to Sissy.

"Mother, I can't! Not now!" Sissy feared another expense. Death and burial could not factor at the moment, already muddled in adjustments. With three children gone from the nest, she seemed uncertain. Sissy thought her children should have what she never had, stability in the suburbs. Her children had no clue on instability but would learn, as people do.

Healthy but for colds and flus from low immunity on franchise food, the kids were okay. Sissy didn't cook; that pendulum swung the other way. She seemed restless by nature, but then relaxing with the family, our family, had changed.

Sissy was expert in her avocation, toy cars.

I tried to comprehend but could not.

Brother explained: "Boring people get together with their toy cars and talk about them."

"That's what people do," I said.

"Yeah. It gets them out with other people, talking. These people wouldn't go without the toy cars."

Mother said Sissy came to Brother's on Saturdays to see Ethel, because people have fewer problems with dogs than with other people.

"She comes over to see Ethel?" I had asked.

"Yes," Mother affirmed. She'd hit the wall on filial devotion and could not reconcile Sissy's as less than her own. Mother kept the blinders in place.

"Looks like a two-pack at the cemetery, Ma." Brother ended our talk of eternity. His coffee cup said: I ♥ being Black. Each teacher at Brother's school got one. He'd ordered another case of cups, just for fun: I ♥ being White. He'd chatted with the board lawyer before handing out his cups. He said his position at school was more secure since last month, when the assistant district superintendent told all faculty and staff to forget old prejudices and animosities and simply get along. "I'm not kidding around," she'd chided. "And that goes for the Blacks, the whites and the Jews!"

VII

FREEZE FRAME

The morning passed on another meal, talk of burial sites, inner-city school politics, mindless TV and nary a mention of the trial, coming right up.

At noon, Sissy said she didn't appreciate Brother and me plying her son with drugs.

Brother asked if she expected us to smoke the dirt weed that little punk brought home from college.

I announced a side trip. I would go in two days, and it would take two days. I said Mother could join me, if she wanted.

She looked up.

Sissy looked up, interrupted and impatient.

Brother nodded, also tracking dates and unspoken histories.

I would drive Mother's car to Southern Indiana the next day.

Mother asked, "Why? We have so much to do."

We had nothing to do but plan the next seven days times three meals times six courses times different grocery stores for coupons and specials. Mother said we'd be in a mad rush without gallivanting around the countryside. So why now?

"It's thirty years," Brother said.

Mother had forgotten.

Sissy either forgot or kept it to herself. Thirty years Monday since our old man died, thirty years since being there.

Brother went back after eighteen years, in his sorting phase. I don't know what he did. I didn't know what I would do but on a homing instinct said, "It's time."

Mother could not make a trip like that without planning. It could take weeks.

I said fine, I'd go alone. Or, she could call Flossie's son and tell him Flossie could croak tomorrow with no ass-wipe on hand. That way, Mother could join the gallivant. I would stay at Aunt Aileen's, because some places are still okay to drop in for a stay after thirty years.

"I don't know," Mother said, obliquely, mentally on her way. She called Aileen an hour later in a huff and a yak over swooping down on Southern Indiana.

Aileen said, slow and easy, "Okay. I'll have some of the girls over for lunch."

"How can you plan a luncheon in one day?"

"Be here by noon," Aileen said calmly, unchanged.

"She's crazy," Mother said. "She thinks she can plan a luncheon in one day."

"Do you think she can?" I asked.

"We have to be there by noon!" Mother said. "Now move!"

Twenty hours and eighteen courses later, after many phone calls on logistics, Mother and I were on the road. We took hard-boiled eggs, lox, bagels, jelly, cream cheese and coffee cake to fend off starvation. Mother said we were looking down the barrel of a long, strenuous day, so eat! She packed fruit, chips, cookies, and chicken she'd fried last night, like old times, riding the train to Flossie's from Southern Indiana.

We got a baby duck or two every year at springtime. We loved our ducks and made duck houses, fed them and gave swimming lessons in the kitchen sink. We took them on the train because a baby duck can't be left alone. The old man never rode the train to Flossie's but couldn't very well take care of baby ducks, ducks having stolen so many baits.

We knew where he stood on ducks.

Brother and I put them in shoe boxes with air holes, grass bedding, a jar lid of water and another jar lid of snacks. We put the boxes in the baggage car, no pets allowed on the train. Once out of the station, we headed back to baggage and our peeping ducks, the water and food shmushed into the grass. They peeped happily, playing in the aisles, and if the conductor allowed, we took them to our seats for cookies and chips. The world was a better place, not so crowded or secure and much more fun.

Some ducks stood out over the years, like Duck-a-Luck, who followed and got upset when his kids rode off on bicycles. Matzo Ball scarfed a matzo ball and got his name. Quacky lived in the kitchen in a box with windows, to look out and see the world. He once saw a crate of strawberries the old man brought home, traded for a mess of bass with a guy who had a strawberry farm on a lake. Quacky stretched his neck for what could have been the last time, reaching for a two-pint snack.

Already blood-red to his belly, his little quack regretting the bulge, Quacky was guilty as charged. But we jumped to, uncrated the berries, ditched the shmush, cleaned and cut the rest for the shortcake Mother already kneaded on the counter.

We didn't fool anyone. "Goddamn fucking ducks," the old man grumbled at the door, seeing Quacky, red in the face and green in the gills. Not to worry; fresh strawberries over shortcake made short work of short fuses.

Quacky had to move outside, fine with him. He'd grown, and the drain field out back remained leaky. Quacky loved his puddle. Red stains turned green, and peace prevailed. He got hosed off to come back in to play when the old man was gone fishing or drinking or hustling a buck or two.

We moved away from the house on the lake in '57 or '59 and after that took our grown ducks to other lakes, where they took a few days to merge into the pecking order.

The old man scored a .22 rifle when I was eleven, swapped a guy for a diamond, so his boys could learn to shoot. We went one summer day to a distant lake, huge and known for catfish, bass, bluegill and many ducks.

I proved a natural, hitting a half-dollar propped on a dandelion at thirty yards.

Brother cried, "Lucky!"

But I hit a bottle cap on the fly, and the old man lit up when I wanted a tougher target and asked, "Can I shoot a duck?"

"Sure!" He sensed an ally in the war against ducks. Sixty yards out, just off a bank, a duck slid into the notched V. I brought her even with the barrel tip, exhaled softly and squeezed, like shooting a duck was no different than snatching a cattail. The gun held seventeen rounds, longs, for range and accuracy. But the hammer clicked empty. Tingles rushed in, like God, saying I'd nearly killed someone.

The rifle settled. The old man took it from me for the reload and gave it back. "Come on, Hotshot, let's see what you got."

I didn't want to.

He said don't worry; our ducks were over to the right.

"No. I don't want to." It wasn't the sort of thing the old man could accept, so I went to diversion, saying I wanted to shoot another half-dollar while Brother held it, you know, out to the side. "I can do it. I won't miss. Pulleeze!" That turned things around on a reprieve for all parties.

"Nah. We better not."

We went home, Brother and I sharing a sigh of relief. I realized that a gun is like a paintbrush that makes a person see everything in need of painting.

Recollecting ducks, youth and growth moments, the road back to Southern Indiana picked up where we'd left off. I'd grown to love animals more than people, much of that love learned or inherited from Mother, who nearly swooned on hearing of my request. She sounded familiar, calling me crazy. "I only wanted to shoot it from his fingertips. It wasn't like we would have propped it on top of his head." She shook her own head, gazing out the window. "I didn't shoot a duck."

The roads from Muzzuhrruh to Hoosierville also showed what humanity was good for. It wasn't like old times. The train was gone to four-lane highway, barren swaths to either side, unnatural habitat where nothing sprouted but franchise signs: Food, Fuel, Lodging. Garish and ugly stuff crowded the frozen landscape.

We ate and remembered how it used to be.

We arrived late, after noon, so the girls were three cups ahead on their drug of choice, caffeine. The mile-a-minute yak was nonstop, like the train used to be, or maybe more like stock car races on a figure-8. The girls, early seventies to mid-eighties, had been the women of my youth. With much ado, they said Mother looked beautiful, lovely and so on, as aging people do. Mother soaked it up. I knew they'd turn to me, turn on me, for rotisserie review.

Rose Sugarman had been married to Al for many years, until he split and died. Rose at eighty-three looked like George Burns. Brother went steady with her daughter Bitzie in eighth grade, a few years before Al split.

Rabbi M got caught *schtuping* a woman at the Holiday Inn, Wednesdays. It had gone on for years with a cover story about study with the monks at St. Meinrad's Monastery. Yeah, studying the function at the junction. Rabbi M got the ax before the old man died and didn't make it to the funeral. M had a five o'clock shadow like eighty-grit sandpaper and chewed on a stogie to muffle his mumbling. Rabbi M was unloved, except for his liaison, a Sunday school teacher who served it on a platter.

Not born Jewish but married into it, she'd converted, down to the *mikvah* or ritual bath. The tradition is disgusting to some, a big shared tub reserved for women in menses. It demonstrates commitment or something the old men deem necessary.

The women, these women, didn't accept her; something about her. She fucked the rabbi for revenge, demonstrating something more or less.

The Inquisition had been at Rose and Al's house, because Al was president of the congregation. *Do you now or have you ever craved shiksa pussy?*

It wasn't that craven but close.

The woman claimed vindictive motivation. Everyone suspected deeper needs, especially the rabbi's wife, Bernice, who asked in authentic *kvetch*, "Monks? What, with the monks? What does he need from the monks, every Wednesday like clockwork, what? Three years?" She'd sent a private detective, who followed to the Holiday Inn. She cried over her misfortune.

We'd giggled over the gossip and M's downfall, but a lifetime later I found a letter from him, sent a few weeks after my *bar mitzvah*, apologizing for his absence. He'd heard it was splendid and known it would be, and that I would carry the honor, tradition, faith and so on. It was a touch of schmaltz but a heartfelt sentiment overall. What a great guy, and who could blame him; Bernice was skinny and shrill. And maybe the craven shiksa got into his heart and warmed it up.

Back down the rabbit hole of long ago, near the north bank of the Oh Hi Oh in Hoosierville, Rose said, "Remember Bitzie? She's married. Divorced. Married with a few kids." Rose made sense intermittently. It didn't matter. She turned to another point, wagging a finger, "No, no, no! It was a serving dish, a glass serving dish!"

The girls looked away.

Rose was confused, so Dora moved closer, to help her. Rose married Mannie Levitz when Al split. Mannie's wife had died, and his sister Dora made the match. "Why not, after schmoozing for sixty years?" Rose and Dora became sisters-in-law. Dora listened, because Rose took good care of her brother Mannie.

"She married a wealthy man from Terre Haute," Rose said.

"Was he Jewish?" Dora asked, turning to me, winking; she had no clue who Rose was talking about.

"Oh, yeah!" Rose said. "She never had no trouble." Rose stopped, seeing me for the first time. "He knew about that basement. You think I'd let him get away with that?" Without context or meaning, Rose rambled. I'd known alternate realities. This was deep space.

"Not for a minute," I said.

She nodded, "Yeah. That bastard Al tried it more than once."

"Hard to believe," I said.

"I told her; they got that big fellow out there to take care of her. You know who I mean . . . Jack . . . Jack . . ."

Dora cut in, "Nobody knows what you're talking about." Dora turned to me, "You look wonderful!" Those not yet dead expressed the sentiment of survival in a small town. Dora made me feel old. None of these women ever said I looked wonderful thirty years prior.

"Jack . . . Big fellow."

"Jake," I said. "Big Jake."

"Yeah! That's the one! Big Jake! I told her!" Rose laughed.

Mother soaked up praise on her children and primed the pump for more. "You should see the grandchildren," she said.

Dora was seventy-two. "I'm so glad you're here. Rose drives me crazy. I can't be with her by myself." She smiled on a sigh.

Henrietta Nussbaum saw the opening and made her move, with a walker but spritely, a geriatric pixie reflecting life in the region, eighty pounds and a head of orange hair spun like cotton candy. Two steps out, she said, "I got a girl for you. Twenty-nine, all of a sudden, available. Nice, huh? And is she a little beauty? Let me tell you something. My granddaughter graduated college and went back and got her master's degree, because she's smart, that one. She goes down to Texas and goes in a bar and sees this fellow and likes his looks, you know, and then sees he has a pin from STD—no . . . SDT, and she goes up and asks him if he's Jewish. Oh, it matters. It does to my grandchildren . . ."

They got married, had babies and he died of lymphoma. The granddaughter was available. Any interest?

"You said twenty-nine. Now she's thirty-one with two kids. That's too old. And the baggage?" I was born in the region and still fluent; a quick solution would more likely stick.

Rose laughed across the room, "Ha! That's right. Who needs it? Listen, Mannie taught me everything about sex! That bastard Al didn't do nothing!"

Jennifer stepped in to murmur, "Lunch ready."

A lovely time it was or would be, with concerns mitigated over Jennifer, server and dishwasher. Jennifer's mama had worked years for Aileen. Jennifer followed in her mama's footsteps. She had two kids and a third due. Jennifer was twenty and big, and the girls wondered if she'd washed her hands.

"I don't think she washed her hands."

"No."

"No, I don't either."

"What? Washed her hands?"

"No, she didn't. She didn't wash her hands."

They shut up when Aileen called into the kitchen, "Jennifer. Wash your hands, Honey."

More coffee fueled the spirit, still at each other's throats, after all these years. I eased back as the girls moved to the lovely-grandchildren competition, Instamatic snaps flying like two-deck pinochle in the old days.

Soon it was gee, it's great to see you. You look terrific. Bye. Aunt Less left first. She'd married Nardy, Adolph's son. Adolph, the old man's oldest brother, died before I was born. Less wasn't Jewish, didn't speak the dialect of cutthroat love and enjoyed indifference at all levels, making her lovable, her smile and independence leaving the room in a lull.

Rose and Dora left in a dither and a spew of hugs, kisses and compliments and boy oh boy oh boy, you oughta see this one or that one or the other one now! That exit also brought a sigh.

Henrietta Nussbaum said, "I think she's lost her marbles."

"They're different colors, that's for sure," Aileen said.

"You ought to talk to her," Mother said. "Tell her, slow and nice. Tell her we don't know what she's talking about."

"She don't hear a damn thing," Aileen said.

"And I don't talk to her," Henrietta said.

"Then talk to Dora," Mother said. "I could talk to Dora."

"Oh, no!" Sylvia said. "You say one word to Dora, she'll blow up. Not one word."

"Let me tell you something," Henrietta said. "Rose and I are the same age, born the same day. We're eighty-three. She was born in the morning, I was in the afternoon, and I look at her and think, 'Am I like that?' I don't think so. I'm intelligent . . ."

"Mm."

"Yes."

"Yes, you are . . ." The polite refrain felt soft, but Henrietta achieved consensus.

"I can talk to people," Henrietta said. "She's nuts!"

"Mm."

"Yes . . . Nuts."

"She's . . ."

It was Henrietta Nussbaum's time to leave. She told me to get the door and carry her things and get the car door, too. At the car, she said I could call her granddaughter, if I wanted to.

I told her I'd be back in Hawaii in a few days. Her granddaughter could call me there.

She scoffed in a cotton-candy flourish, got in and drove off.

I waved goodbye, such a small town, after all.

Back inside, Aunt Aileen was saying, "She's a mean one."

Mother nodded.

Sylvia concurred on Henrietta's meanness. Just before Milton died the year before, Henrietta failed to offer a ride to a social function, knowing Sylvia needed a ride, what with Milton sick and about to die.

Sylvia scooted to the edge to tell of Milton's last days and months, up to the sad decision for lethal antibiotic injection. He died, but the story went on. The doctors knew nothing of the exotic disease that killed Milton. They wanted to remove his brain, for science. The family approved.

Slogging through ten more minutes, Sylvia followed Milton's brain on its farewell tour. It drew many esteemed doctors, arriving at last in Cincinnati . . .

The phone rang.

Mother had nodded off.

Aileen picked up.

I went for a whiz.

Sylvia went on to Dayton, Cleveland and around the bend on keeping a kosher home. She kept kosher for years, for Milton, but no more, and she didn't care. She still slept till ten, but it wasn't the same, waking up without toast and juice on the nightstand. Milton did that for her, all those years. Finally, Sylvia stood.

Mother woke.

Aileen got off the phone.

I came back.

Sylvia said farewell and waddled out.

"She's so full of shit," Aileen said. "I swear."

I laughed.

Aunt Aileen wasn't our aunt, nor was Uncle Louie our uncle, not in the blood sense. But their house was also home. I don't know how we got intertwined, except for Mother's need. Aileen stayed cool when Mother got hot, calm when Mother got tense, alkaline to Mother's acidic. As yin to Mother's yang, Aileen stayed even-keeled. She had no moods, except for occasional cravings, like buttermilk or fried chicken.

Aunt Aileen's house hadn't changed, a little place in a country neighborhood with a barn, a garden, a blackberry hedge and a few giant trees. I laughed at the years and her enduring skill at calling a spade a spade.

"I have an idea for dinner," I said. "We'll go out, on me, somewhere we won't be seen."

They laughed, and Mother and I had finally arrived.

The afternoon was short and gray, cold and misty. It fell into night like dirt in a hole. Dinner was a push, too much, but Mother and Aileen enjoyed going out, and how often did I come to town? I stayed up late, reading, auditing old times, names, faces, fun and games, coming home, really home.

We played Hide and Seek in this house, hid under this bed, in that closet. I complained at Red Rover and Crack the Whip; I was too small. Red Rover was only capture for me, and I hated the tail end of the whip. Freeze Tag and Piggy Wants a Wave were better.

We put lightning bugs in jars and let them go in that room in the dark. I doused the light, but got no twinkle, and recall felt lifeless as a disinterment. An image here, a yelp there, a call out and . . . stillness. Recollection sorted like a museum exhibit, preserved, with no pulse.

I remembered tomorrow, thirty years ago.

Mother was up at six to get an early start. She stood in the door till I opened my eyes. "Are you up? Let's go. Did you bring warm clothes? What do you want for breakfast?"

"Yes, I did. But it won't be that cold."

"That's what you think." She headed down the hall, knowing what I needed for breakfast. "It's cold in July in a cemetery." Pearls of wisdom, quirks of nature she imparted unto me, lo though she leaned on seventy-four.

And there it was, a January morning, gray, stillborn, crushed with cold, flecked with sleet on a fluky breeze that wheezed and would give up the ghost in a few hours. Sunrise looked like dusk, and so did midmorning, when we found Mt. Sinai Cemetery on the far side of town. Nobody used Mt. Sinai since '65 when the new cemetery on the other side got popular.

I hadn't known what I would do that morning, except to sit, and I'd brought a folding chair from Brother's. I went to get it as Mother and Aileen got out to look over the short wall at the old man's grave. Mother said she couldn't go near it because the Law forbids a divorced woman to approach her ex-husband's grave.

Aileen said, "Uh huh."

"You approached it thirty years ago," I said.

"I didn't know then," she said. "Besides, I couldn't let you kids go alone."

"So now you know," I said. "So what? If your heart is clear, and you want to approach, you can." I spoke like I knew best, and she smiled, seeing the man in me, though I'd hit middle age before she could let go of the child. But no, she could not approach the grave.

Watching me pull my folding chair from the trunk, she asked, "What are you doing?"

It was a process I'd learned in my newest home, a continent and ocean away. It was nothing and everything. I would meditate, empty the vessel to make room for contact, not with things, beings or events, but ambient. I would relinquish rationale and lose coordinates in order to sense places and times in essence, removing those things from thingness. Could I explain this to Mother? I thought not, knowing what she would say. I smiled.

She waited. An answer was required, just as I'd felt my presence required, requiring the aggravation of modern travel, because being in certain places at certain times requires the gauntlet of long flights, long drives, excessive nostalgia, wasted hours and harsh weather.

Snow began to fall. Frost formed on the car windows. A chill rushed in. We trembled, time to proceed, to stay warm in the car for her and Aileen, in the heart for me, like the ice people do. "I'm going to see the Ice King," I said. I didn't think she'd understand but hoped she'd let it pass, one more crazy notion.

She scoffed as she'd often scoffed. You talk so crazy, she was about to say but held back, remembering the morning thirty years to the day, that the dam broke, flooding Mt. Sinai and the hearts and eyes gathered there. She remembered her baby's pain and sought again to comfort. Tolerance displaced her need to comprehend. Uncertain but accepting, she came up with a new look, a half-smile of anguish.

"The Ice King," I repeated, fending off distraction, because meditation begins best before it begins. I'd taken the first step, folding chair in hand, seeking calmness in urgent cold and the focus of no focus. "I'm going to the frozen north," I more or less reminded myself, "where spirits live."

Mother's look twisted, either from her grasp to understand or reaching her limit.

"To express gratitude," I said, past explanation.

Aileen laughed short, remembering the old man as Mother did, as rough and sometimes dangerous. Aileen likely thought I should be grateful for surviving, shaking her head at the old man's son.

She and Louie had helped Mother on the day of Exodus from the land of bondage in '61, had picked up Brother and me at school and taken us to the new house, a small rental on Congress Avenue. She and Louie had gone home and turned out the lights, knowing the wrath to follow. It didn't matter thirty years later.

Uncle Louie understood uniquely that the volatile side would go off if shaken, so best not shake it. They weren't close friends, Louie and the old man, but got along, as small-town people do. Louie was also big, fat where the old man was thick and powerful. He smoked cigars and called the old man Puddin'. He also survived, the maestro of stirring some shit just right.

The old man called him Puddin' back and let the peace be.

Mother said Louie was as much a troublemaker as the old man was crazy.

Country Jews who knew grim history didn't conform to stereotype but knew the score. They didn't profile like shtetl Jews of Europe but adapted to America, forgoing idiom and dialect as a means to frame a culture. They factored the score, however, there on the Ohio River, as Jews anywhere will do, sooner or later. Never again.

A community endured, rich and poor, Jews who knew what the world can do. They didn't worry about it, but Indiana Jews understood the irony upon them, casual lives notwithstanding. God told Abraham, *Kill your son as a sacrifice.* It was a test, ham-handed but apparently necessary, and Abraham went along, in faith, ready to gut the kid, until God said, *Okay, okay, don't kill him. I'm not that kind of God. This was a test, so I could see.*

That part of it seems odd. What does God not see? Never mind. God advised that sins should be expunged without human sacrifice. *Use a goat.* Just so, the chosen people imparted their troubles unto a scapegoat. Then came irony.

Pliant and easily contained, Jews also became scapegoats. Pogrom (po•GROM, massacre of Jews in eastern Europe by hostile gangs, usually Cossacks on horseback) could soothe economic woes, restore a king, vent pressure and please the populace. For centuries, Jews couldn't own land in much of Europe, when agriculture yielded wealth. Restricted to lowly pursuits, like scribes, minstrels, analysts and, most unsavory, money lenders, they adapted. Success led to Weimar Germany.

Hoosierville Jews, like Jews of old, were rural folk. Like modern folk, they fit in, no shtetls required. A fourth *Reich* wasn't likely in Southern Indiana or anywhere in the USA. But American hero Charles Lindberg was best pals with A. Hitler and ran for president.

In 1961, I was ordered to kneel and pray to Jesus in the church across the road from school. I refused to kneel and failed eighth grade for a few days, until Mother and a makeshift commando crew enforced the rule.

Chief Justice Earl Warren and the Supreme Court affirmed the rule on separation of church and state. Original precepts of the Constitution should not change for zealots. A public school system would not tolerate religion or Christian persecution.

The old man also enforced the rule, Jewish enough to know the score and discuss it as necessary.

Uncle Louie wasn't too religious, but Aileen said he'd raised hell on his deathbed, when they shaved him on a Saturday. I hadn't thought much of observance till then but stopped shaving on Saturdays to remember Louie and rules. Much of Judaism is remembering, lest we forget.

Aileen had shaken her head, as I told Mother of the frozen north and a cockamamie king. She and Louie said from way back, "That boy's wild. You'll never keep him home."

And so it came to pass. So what? I'd gone out and come around thirty years to the day, to explain a situation. I didn't need to and didn't need pressing at the old man's grave. I cut both old ladies some slack in mutual tolerance and offered my own look on a short laugh. What would I do at my father's grave? *Just you watch. And listen.* I didn't explain, sparing Mother from further questions. *What do you mean, meditate?* And I spared myself from yelling like the old man, who never figured it out like I did.

I carried my chair down the wall to the entrance and into the old man's place. Unfolding at the foot, I sat, feet on the ground, back straight, chest open, shoulders floating, palms on thighs.

Thirty years ago, I'd stood in the rain. Rain warms the air. I'd bundled up for bitter cold, but in that place, cold trickled in, saturating to the bone. A living body reacted with trembling. I brought the universe in by half, and half again and again to the center, freeing mind of rationale, of cause and effect, letting go the pain. So what? Controlled, steady breathing was what.

But simple technique does not grant simple results; the shakes got bad, like spin cycle, off-balance, and Death rose on a dark fibrillation, a presence among the living.

Is it time? Death inquired, eager and attentive as a perfect host in a cemetery.

Surrounded by forebears whose legacy is me, I had no fear. I could not stop the rattle or make contact in a minute or two. Death and I remained patient. I sat through phase 1 hypothermia, breathing in the positive sense, leveling, but not like those around me. I laughed, in life, having come so far.

In through the nose, out through the mouth, deep, slow and slower, breathing calmed. Ripples faded, like a pond before freezing. In a while, as if placated, the shakes went away. The host settled and things, such as they were, went beyond pain, even for the living. A body eased into being of no being, flesh and bones finding the better stillness.

Communion came as a neutral presence, with whom things are known, omniscience is breathed, in which questions and answers are given, one and the same.

I watched a man on a folding chair by his father's grave, back straight, hands folded, tears rolling, not like a kid drenched in grief but as a player in a scene of death and life. Bitter cold made those tears, not sadness, and new shakes were timed with new flurries.

Some men don't want to cry, because forty-three is far from thirteen. Just so, the tears slowed but tracked another pain, a trail of ice. And the gates opened, free and clear, anything ever wanted, forward or back, audience with the king.

Consequence is for the living, if they want it—that was the gist. The dead are beyond, though spirits linger or seem to, receptive to information: *I sailed two oceans and rode a motorcycle across Europe.*

Mother is taken care of.

I got a chicken named Flossie and a farm in the country, two acres of beauty with avocado trees and mangos, papayas, lemons, bananas, oranges, grapefruit, tangerines, mac nuts, lichee, guava and trees yielding color like a cash crop. Screaming yellow crotons with blood-red veins, bauphinia, jatropha, euphorbia, giant white birds of paradise, little blue and orange birds, pink hibiscus and red and white, red, white, orange and orange red and red orange and more blood-red, gardenias, pikake, plumeria and jasmine with sweet scent to bend your knees, and ducks and chickens, palm trees and . . . a good life, good weather, an ocean . . .

And sometimes it's too much, so nice you want to hang out all the time, but I'm too young to be a hermit and ain't been out in a while. So I headed out and thought I'd stop by . . .

Sentiment surfaced, regrettably unshared until those few minutes more. Like in '59, when the old man came home one afternoon to lie on the bed, as down as ever before. He had two years left. I came to the bed to show a new toy, something I'd invented, and he said to come, lie with him. I did, knowing better than to talk, until he moaned. "I got to find some money. I got to. I don't know what to do."

I sat up. "I know! A guy on the radio said no matter what, he'd lend twenty-five hundred dollars to anybody!"

He'd half-smiled and looked sadder still, and I knew the guy on the radio was one more lying sonofabitch.

I'd give you the dough right now if . . . you know . . .

I laughed again, thinking a check would be better than cash. Laughter is a lifeline. And the money didn't matter anymore. But the idea was big and needed sharing.

I scrambled hard and fell plenty, got back up, brushed off and jumped back in, as required in our line of work. A good chin helps; I learned that. It comes from no alternative and makes you tough. Thanks for the whiskers and the stamina to take a few. I got lucky on a winner and parlayed and waited steady and went inside to score again for life in enviable conditions that would have looked unbelievable back then.

The message mattered. The old man was romantic in the rough-and-tumble tradition. He loved westerns, good guys and bad guys, right and wrong, no pussyfooting around, not with simple truth close at hand. Adventure and nature were the legacy and flashed like life.

At depth in a stiff current with sharks, the ocean groaning and creaking like old bones seeking a comfortable position to lie in, relaxing into the flow and kindred spirits felt good.

Big scooters over the Alps and Pyrenees, up and down both coasts and across two deserts on a horse with no name.

Selling twenty-four condos in six weeks on a wing and a prayer and iffy bank financing in flipflops and shorts made me think of you, navigating the straits to get clear of the storm.

A business rising from ashes to summitry on a five-hundred-dollar charge to a credit card was better than Ashland Oil, cleaner and more fun.

Who could have known, so long ago? Maybe they imagined, given the will and the wild gene. Memories crowded in.

Oh, and death seemed closer than now, waves breaking at the spreaders, their faces haggard and frothing, not peaceful like here and a long way from Miami in '55 at the Gould Hotel . . . Remember?

I could. Futzing for days at the shallow end, ready for more, I saw the old man in the shade, in shoes and pants, grumbling over a highball, the goddamn heat, too many fucking hotels and people. I walked up, dripping. "I wanna swim." He got it: swimming happened at the deep end. And he liked straight talk from a guy at three-six, thirty-eight pounds.

"Okay, go on down there." He gave the deep end a half nod.

I went.

"Get closer."

I stepped to the edge.

"Jump in."

I jumped.

"Now swim."

That was it, clean and concise as the old one-two.

Mother saw and jumped up, screaming bloody murder and crazy for a few hours more. Left to her, I'd still be shallow. "What's wrong with shallow. Who needs it so deep?"

But I swam like a natural. I'd seen Tarzan swim with crocodiles! I could do it. The old man would have saved me, anyway, but I hate to conjure that scene, with the pants and shoes and a highball.

Risk was a common chord, compassion another. When the old man started up in diamonds and carried a gun, Mother called him crazy. But one night we pulled onto the shoulder behind some drunk boys in a stalled car. One yelled and walked back with a tire iron but got polite, looking down the little black hole of eternity. The old man said, "Thought we'd help you boys out. Need a lift?"

The drunk boy said nothing.

"Suit yourself." We pulled back onto the road. I was a kid but got the picture: crazy and compassionate with a slight lean.

Back at the Gould, we took a break to walk down Collins Avenue to Walgreen's. It felt more like a reprieve from the noise than a celebration. Call it luck or synchronicity, we walked in and way back to a very small display of masks, fins and snorkels. He picked a set from the high end, with a ping-pong ball snorkel. He had a notion, as parents can, but this felt out of the blue.

Life changed.

Back at the beach, I sloshed in the shallows, amazed at mud minnows and sand crabs, at a world unimagined, rendering stick pretzels and Nickel Nips as nothing.

He'd got it right and got a charge out of that, wingtips soaked, grinning, no goddamns or sonsabitches in that action. "What do you see, Hotshot?"

A small crab waved a claw in greeting, and I sputtered up, "You can see everything!"

Remember?

I remembered once in '56, around in there, the old man wanted to go fishing, a commitment of six or eight hours, and a kid could get bored in one. I went; he sorely liked the company. We headed way out and stopped at a country store for sodas and chips, bread and mustard and the cheapshit pimento loaf we loved but never got at home. I paid, to get comfortable handling money. I went about fifty pounds by then. The guy at the register looked up. "Well, sonny, out with Grampa today?"

Oh, Christ. The old man stepped up for a fistful of shirt and pulled the guy close. "I'll Grampa you, you sorry sonofabitch." Testy, sensitive to suggestion that he'd done it wrong, having a kid at fifty and going broke, he reacted.

Mother called it crazy.

The scene made sense to a kid having fun. But the guy behind the counter didn't seem like a bad guy. He just didn't know and had to learn. He came up for review, graveside, for another laugh at the piss and vinegar on tap. The shakes came and went again.

The old man had a phrase for tough times, between a shit and a sweat. That was another laugh; a few words that could frame life in pathos. He wasn't alone. A TV hero of those days, Chester

A. Riley in *The Life of Riley*, sized things up more politely, "What a revoltin' development this is."

The old man comprehended conventional society but resisted; too crowded and constrained, and him rambunctious. Me, too, but pop-in-the-nose diplomacy got outdated fast.

The heart attack in Oklahoma City took him. He'd followed Florence and John to help with aluminum siding sales. Uncle John was done building bridges in South America, soft talk for the slammer, for bilking folks on aluminum siding. Back in action, he'd figured out how to avoid mistakes.

Florence died in '72. I was in South Carolina, where she sent me a watch, "a real nice one, Honey, because a man should have a nice-looking watch, so people can know." She sent fifty bucks besides and called it mad money. She said I shouldn't save it or spend it sensibly. I'd heard she wasn't doing well and called to say hey. She appreciated the contact, still confused on Mother's vibe. Florence had long nails way before fake nails, bright red, and a high coif. Thick like the old man, she offset in heels, a chiffon dressing gown and a cigarette holder. She played mahjong with the girls and called everyone Honey.

Uncle John did well in aluminum siding until heading down to South America. He could hit a mark in stride on a glittering line. He loved the horses and drove his Caddy to Miami— Hialeah. He thought the starter track in Kentucky was perfect for Brother and me, but Hialeah was Mecca to him. "Oh, golly. I'm telling you. It's marvelous. And the cheese bullintzes! Simply marvelous." He loved the action and felt triumphant at Hialeah, a racetrack that served bullintzes, meaning *blintzes*. He said marvelous or gargeous, meaning gorgeous. What a hambone, but when Brother and I laughed like hyenas, he joined in, knowing we thought the material marvelous.

Uncle John kept a box of paper placemats in his trunk, showing *The Last Supper*. He gave them to friends, mostly in Miami, like calling cards, making much ado over the personal note, handwritten at the bottom.

1/1/1

Dear Irving,

The herring in sour cream was delish! The bagels had to be from New York. The knishes were like Mama's, the matzo balls light as goose feathers. The kreplach was out of this world, the tzimmes and farfel divine. Oy gott! The brisket! Not since Miami Beach have I tasted kugel like that. And the cheese blintzes . . . Oy vayizmere!

Your pal,

Jesus H. Christ

"Ha! Ha, ha! So? Does a Jew know from deli, or doesn't He? Ha!" Last Supper placemats were Uncle John's signature schtick, and he presented many, writing the note at the bottom every time and laughing like the joke was fresh. The last of the 50s big-fins outlaws, he wore fabulous rings and watches and kept the Caddy miles ahead of repo. Colorful, garish and loud, when he wasn't in South America, he shone on 24-karat bullshit.

Lying beside Florence at Mt. Sinai, he still seemed cheerful on the frigid breeze: *what er ya gonna do? It ain't so bad.* And forgivable, having waded many puddles to the money on the other side. By aluminum siding redux in Oklahoma, John and the old man were down to wits and willpower, doing what they could. Uncle John never held a gun to anybody and made people laugh. I met plenty worse guys of lesser ilk, moody, hurtful, unstable and hazardous. Not him.

Only last week, thirty years ago, Brother and Sissy and I got home from school to find Mother waiting, constrained.

I set my books down and shrugged off another wasted day.

She smiled sadly, tearful, and I knew. "Your father died."

But I already knew.

Things keep sorting.

That bone-cold January morning in the Midwest made it plain to see how thirty years dead could mellow a guy out, could allow personal development, postmortem. Common ground held no anger, revenge, fists or fight.

A reckoning rose.

I felt the clan—beckoned the clan—infused their memory with compassion and dispatch. We would reconcile, quick and clean. War cries would rise, hearts to sky.

He knew. They all knew: Izzy, Rudy, Sammy and Hazel, Adolph, Ben, Florence and John. The parents, Haddie and Joe.

Knowing was in the rational sense of the living, my sense, but in spirit, it passed at last to the skinny kid grown up, on his own. At forty-three, he could throw a punch and take a few.

Resolution at Mt. Sinai was another epitaph, not cast in stone but marking time and ending the safe passage that guardian angels provide. It felt good, a natural transition, fortifying, like a new adventure. The child became father to the man . . .

Go . . . now . . .

Rest in peace.

The shakes came on flurries, the host growing restless for a check-in. I, the living, had stayed too long, colder than a living person should be for forty minutes. I stood to utter what nobody there needed but the living should say, "Thank you."

I folded my chair. Mother and Aileen waited, restless to go, and they let me go, too, without the usual questions.

We drove to Newburgh, the riverfront, where hole-in-the-wall places had sold crawdads, crickets, night crawlers, minnows, meal worms, hooks, line, nets, Nehi Soda, lunch meat, white bread, Moon Pies, stick pretzels, jaw breakers, rope licorice, bubble gum, Nickel Nips and more stuff than a kid could take in. The walk down to the rocky banks had led to the old guys who knew the river, coming and going, fishing for carp and monster cats. They were gone, but it felt like life thirty years before.

At a semi-chic bistro back up on the renovated waterfront strip, among wannabe-chic antique stores and generic-chic boutiques, I imagined a chic bait shop with svelte crawdads, pastel crickets, fashionable nightcrawlers and mud minnows. Nothing decrepit remained, Nehi Soda and Moon Pies, catfish stew and black coffee, mustard, bread and lunch meat had gone to fa-fa dishes with fey names meant to be marvelous. Best the old man never saw this.

At least the bistro was Hoosier chic, with catfish *à l'orange*, a country-bred waitress who presented the specialties of the *maison* and a second-floor view of the widest, deepest, swiftest river of my youth. Its banks frozen, swirls and eddies rushing southwest, it looked dead but alive, freezing but boiling, still hell-bent for leather like some of the boys who grew up nearby.

We ate, took Aileen home and backtracked to St. Louis on more of the past and another hard lesson for Mother from her most demanding teacher, me.

She remembered again, befitting the moment, in case the outing and sentiment might lead poor, naive me to the wrong conclusion. The circumstance, one more time, had been dire; no money for milk for her children . . .

I broke in. "Say what you will. Blood won't come from stones or turnips. A man with no money has no money. He might still come up with a drink under pressure, because he can count on a drink. And whether you see it or not, I'm in the same business as my father. The only difference is luck. He had it but lost it. I kept it. You should recognize the will, the wits, the drive, tooth and nail, as his. Not to sell you short: the sustenance and nurturing are yours. I owe survival to you. But I cannot tolerate your indictment. I take it personally. I always have. It must stop."

We rode a few hours in silence. She slept, maybe dreaming of the day I'd forgive her shortcomings as I forgave his. She needed a break after a lifetime of cleaning up messes for others.

I resolved to be more generous, to value her unique sense, her idiosyncrasy, her slanted view. I would not criticize. But she was Mother, after all, and I wanted her to get it right. I wanted to get it right, too, watching her sleep as she'd watched me forty years before, in awe and wonder and hope for goodness in life. We got home late.

VIII

BUTTER SIDE UP

The trial was two days later.

I repressed imagery of timing and relaxation, thinking elsewhere instead of measuring distance and staying loose with the jab, jab, jab. I mostly failed. Revenge became worrisome, a nagging compulsion, a pratfall in life. Emotions ran high but felt anticlimactic. We'd already won, more or less.

Anger had festered too long to go away. A clean pop in the nose made sense for all parties, quicker, more concise and better resolved than a legal gauntlet. I thought Flossie's son would prefer a pop in the face over giving so much money back to Mother. Then again, I wanted to throw from the hips, in the stance, to the far side of his skull; back to square one.

I wore a suit from ten pounds earlier, a bit strained, like me, and richly conservative, coffee brown with faint pinstripes and double-breasted, so color and cut matched the old man's suit in a photo from '41, no coincidence. He'd borrowed big to bet on oil fields. He looked confident in that shot, broad-chested in a cashmere overcoat, Stetson hat and no doubts. I'd borrowed big on the future, betting long on revenge one day. I thought of it as justice and still wonder what's the diff.

Moderate oil flow brought money, short of debt service. He lost the show to sideliners waiting to pick it up. Ashland Oil reaped billions. I had also flowed with promise but with a difference, too, cutting losses as necessary to bet another day.

He went into house building, scrambling with new loans. He did okay but spent too much and ended up at the track to make it up. Diamonds glittered but mostly broke even. Package liquor made sense. He knew liquor and had many friends who needed it. Lines blurred on half-pint sales to other hustles to the end.

Instinct runs in a family. Luck favors the bold, but success needs foresight, to see where failure might lurk. That's the rub. Success and failure happen; both are present all the time.

Attitude is not everything. Captain Smith said, "Even God couldn't sink this ship." And *Titanic* left the dock on a maiden and final voyage. God sank it, sending many people down on an attitude of presumption and too few lifeboats.

Every outing needs a backdoor, a bailout, a safety net, lifeboats. What could he do on a huge debt falling short? Failure seemed innate to his assumption that people of goodwill, good nature and plain goddamn sense would favor the key man, the guy with foresight and will. He fucked up.

The oil field photo showed attitude. It doesn't look like a fatal flaw but sank him on a casual brush with an iceberg. Money on hand is nothing. Cash shortfall is everything. He'd been a natural, a winner with vision, but he fell short. He fucked up.

He lost on faith in others to do as he would have done. If he'd loaned money on a project that looked strong but needed more, he would have loaned more. If a friend opened a liquor store, he would have bought cases of liquor. If a friend sold diamonds, he would have bought a few. If a friend was a building contractor, he would have built a house. He valued friendship, and though short of arrogance on assuming it, he fucked up.

The lesson became second nature. We moved six times in nine formative years, downscale, from homes owner-built to houses rented. Instability was a way of life. The old man grew up in one house, maybe too comfortable to see downside potential. But I speculate.

I hadn't worn a suit in years, and double-breasted felt like a vintage movie, playing out. Times had changed, fast-forward upon us, up from ninety-three pounds and five feet tall. I didn't go five-ten, two-twenty but matched his stride, broad-chested, not as thick but just as game. To a fault?

The courtroom double doors felt like steps up to the ring, and I laughed on the way through, imagining the duck under the top rope, ducking back out and back under as many fighters do, for luck or superstition. In the ring, I shook all over, ready to rumble. I'd come to unify the title and knew how to do it. I scanned. Past and future converged. I glared on the opposing corner, not so much a stare down but in disbelief.

Flossie's son, stooped and frail, clung to his stone-face wife. She struggled to support him and her backside. They shrank my need, briefly, until their little charade came clear: looks like, sounds like. He was seventy, not that old; frail, feeble and pitiable were exhibits A, B and C, your honor. Who can win, bullying an old man? Their deception was constant.

I laughed.

To my amazement and gratification, Mother laughed, too, shaking her head, chewing her gum.

"Are they so frail?"

She shook again, this time popping her gum.

We felt good, better than in days, wanting it over. Victory would be Pyrrhic, serving a need way past shelf life. I wished Flossie's son and the Devilment quick and painless death. Vaporization would be best, but there we were. We'd settle for a return of Mother's money. I laughed again.

The Devilment cackled, "Don't laugh!"

Sadly, down to the bickering phase, she'd engaged me. "You look the same inside and out," I said "And your ass. So big."

Her foundation wrinkled and flaked on her signature grimace/grin, eyebrows high, orbs bulging, conspiring against her. She wanted to breathe flames but got only bad breath.

Sissy stepped in to stop the crossfire.

The Devilment had taken the shot on her ass with a duck and weave of her own and drawn me in to where an insult on the old man could have triggered a reaction. Well, a knockout punch would have been gratifying but stoopid, but a bitch slap? Perfect, except for looking like a punch and ending on a mistrial.

Sissy's intervention felt abrupt and necessary. I wouldn't have clocked the Devilment but thought someone should.

Intentions glared, and round one ended, each camp eying the opposite corner.

"She's the cause of it all," Mother said. Nobody said Christ on a crutch or give it a break or put a lid on it. We put a lid on ourselves and let her rant. The in-laws were moving out of our world and would be gone on the task at hand. Mother said, "That bitch won't cook for him or take care of him at all, if you want to know the truth." The Devilment seemed irrelevant to Mother scrubbing floors, making sandwiches, washing, drying, scrimping in deference to them.

We stayed mum. Mother's mind-warp had worsened but worked well for the prosecution.

Brother calmed her, explaining that she'd soon be free of the curse. He got the look for his trouble but went on to explain the first symptom of the curse: anal retention. Flossie's son was constipated, always, like Flossie. Constipation was a way of life. Defecation would deprive them of something no less than a loss of goods paid for. They couldn't let go.

Flossie's son had not aged well, his pointy chin parallel to his pointy beak. Rawhide lips stretched thin from a lifetime of grinning failed to cover crooked yellow teeth. Bent and gray but still twitchy, he looked dead as an old rattler who warranted caution a few hours after leaving the body.

The high ceiling and ornate walls cast the courtroom in hallowed air meant to elevate the judge and the act of judgment. The great one entered, rose to the high seat, did not sit but said, "Counsel. My chambers."

The next two hours dragged, as lawyers argued numbers and claims. Neither side showed much skill. Sly Albertson prattled predictably, restating in-law claims of truth, justice and the American way. Kevin shook his head and mumbled.

They took a break. Kevin debriefed. I extrapolated his headshaking mumbles.

Brother said he'd need to run home before too long to unplug his food dehydrator or lose the load, because the stuff tastes like shit if it dehydrates too long. And he'd paid seven dollars more for rush shipping on a new Snack 'n Sandwich Maker for hot snacks and tasty sandwiches, and, well, forget it; it would need a signature, and he'd miss the UPS guy anyway.

The courtroom was overheated, so all parties retired to the lobby corridor for better air and pacing.

The lawyers reconvened in the judge's chambers.

In two hours more, we declined a low-ball offer to settle, three grand or so. We didn't whoop or holler at having them on the ropes but felt better when Mother laughed short.

I saw a hundred-five thousand as final. I watched the enemy. The clock ticked.

That's all it came to. I still wanted something tangible, even if nuanced, like an inadvertent ankle snag and subtle hip bump to send a wicked man sprawling, to exclaim, "Oh! Sorry." I wanted to watch him try to get up. Or her. Also sad, but okay. I stared and smiled in sheer will of no love. It felt toxic, like tainted Milk of Magnesia, and I sincerely hoped this would be the last of these sorry people.

I couldn't tell if Flossie's son felt the vibe, but he called for the bailiff. "Bailiff!"

The bailiff didn't come.

He called again, in need of help.

I stood.

The bailiff hurried out but couldn't tell why, so he yelled for everyone to settle down.

The lawyers emerged, walked through the courtroom and out to the corridor, where each side confabbed on a revised offer. They'd come up to fifty grand. It felt better, like a jab with snap.

We said no. It was easy.

Mother asked, "Will it be over? Will that be the end of it?"

Oh, she could push my buttons. Overriding her question, I reminded her of spending several thousand dollars, two years on the phone and many hours in airports and planes, working on this. In three hours more, we would have her just reward, not the hundred-five grand stolen but part of it, most of it, if we could stay strong on resolve, relax with fortitude and be true to ourselves. We needed to make the effort . . .

She hung her head. "He's my brother."

It ended.

We drove home at dusk. Fifty grand was a sting and, as Sissy pointed out, a TKO on the gossip line. Mother had sued her brother, Flossie's son, for stealing her share of the rent. She won. He lost, guilty as charged. Moreover, community chatter would be nothing next to the club nitty gritty.

"You wouldn't," Mother said.

"Wouldn't what?" I asked.

She shook her head.

Sissy would. Death by gossip would be more refined and, for them, a more grotesque form of justice.

Brother distracted with a question, straightforward and disarming as Mr. Rogers. "When do you think it all started?"

"1929," Mother said, staring off at a vintage moment, still fresh sixty-two years later. She was eleven. Flossie's son was seven. "We got five cents a week, and I went and got a Hershey Bar. And he took it. He took it!" Stuck on his injustice, she went back to where it all began.

"He took it," Brother repeated to the imaginary crowd gathered round to hear her story. "But did she complain?"

"No," Mother said. "I gave it gladly . . ." She sought more, but the moments jumbled, so many of them rushing in.

"She gave it gladly," Brother said, moving her story along. "And then she asked him how his BM looked. Did he chew good, or could he see the nuts?"

Mother nodded woefully, a giver to a fault, and a fatal flaw it would have been, but for the other side of the family.

At Brother's house, adding nothing to her sparse store of lessons in life, Mother called Flossie to make sure everything was in order, to make sure Flossie got her enema and dinner. They spoke of bodily function.

I asked if I could say hello.

Mother, weakened, sensed restoration of a united front against the world. The curse lingered.

She handed the phone and I said, "Thank God! Thank God, the money is still in the family!"

Mother grabbed it back and said, "I'll be home later." She listened a few seconds more and hung up. "She wants to know when. Sonofabitch."

"Which sonofabitch?" I asked.

"Why doesn't she call her son?" Mother asked.

"Yes," Brother said. "That's a good question. Why doesn't she call her son?"

We had wine with dinner, two bottles. Mother got home way after ten, with an entire glass of wine under her belt.

The following month Flossie moved to a facility, where they promised the enemas, but she complained: too rushed, no grease on the nozzle, too cold and too fast, as if they didn't care.

Mother got her own condo with help from her children.

Sissy became a renowned collector of toy cars and more of the good daughter Mother wanted her to be, if not the best daughter Mother could have imagined.

Mother was mostly grateful, though still challenging her children to "do the right thing," to make nice with the awful people she'd come from.

I reminded her that she'd not been a whole person but an attendant to Flossie since childhood. "You know this but won't change. You may think you've changed. But do you get the respect you deserve?"

"From who?"

"From yourself, for starters."

"You talk crazy," Mother said.

"I suppose I do. Crazy and true."

Flossie finally died on the morning of her ninety-seventh birthday. Mother was distraught, having planned a luncheon with the aunts and cousins on that side. The cooking was done, the cakes baked. "She was looking forward to it," Mother said.

"So?" Brother asked. "She croaked with a party to look forward to. How bad could that be?"

Mother mumbled, "Well . . . She . . . You know . . ."

I didn't visit for Flossie's funeral but went after, for Mother, to ease the transition. At seventy-six in a life of her own, she'd held up, not too wobbly from so many years in bindings. I suggested a visit to the tropics.

She mumbled something and said, "I can. I'm free now."

Brother said Flossie's last fit was the usual breathless convulsion but more compelling. The ambulance came for the dog and pony parade, with the stretcher, the machines, graphs and drip-line drugs. Stabilized in the ambulance, they headed to St. Luke's. But a few blocks out, a medic said no, they should not go to St. Luke's but to St. John. Her doctor was at St. John.

The other medic said no, not St. John, she should go to St. Luke's. He was certain. But they turned around and drove across town to St. John, because the first medic was more certain. But a voice on the radio said they were late at St. Luke's. So they turned around and drove back across town to St. Luke's, siren blaring to marginal effect in traffic. DOA.

Were Flossie's last moments of chaos and runaround a karmic retribution for chaos and runaround? How often do medics argue directions over sirens and traffic? What a way to go, for one so righteous.

Brother was still pleased with his Snack 'n Sandwich Maker and surprised that it made excellent waffles, too, that even the dogs liked with cartoons on Saturday mornings. He resolved to work off the waffles on his new Nordic Track Machine, as seen on TV, hiking cross-country on a boost from his new 2-in-1 Espresso/Cappuccino Machine. He went whole hog on the grinder, too. Fuck it; he was there.

I came in yet again, pondering '00, the year the old man was born. Spirits lingered like smoke. I took some of the old photos. Mother didn't want them, again calling clan bravado false, like the promise; the money never came, nor milk for her children, in case I'd forgotten. I regretted her bitterness, remembering Rudy, Izzy and Sammy for easy dispositions, color and give.

I told her to go have a tongue sandwich and use her own tongue. She hadn't heard that one in a long time and maybe forgot, or not: like father like son. "Ha! Gotcha."

She didn't laugh but asked if I needed flatware for eight, "God-awful ugly stuff." The old man had given it when they got engaged. She never used it but, come to think of it, maybe she would, for Passover, next week! She said it was crazy for me to leave, since I was there already, and she hadn't realized that it would be Passover next week!

I spoke of home responsibilities.

"This is your home!"

"I know what to do when it's time to go. Do you?"

She called me morbid but shut up and let me go.

I stopped in San Francisco to visit friends, as planned. I hadn't remembered Passover, but my friends had friends in Marin who would host the first Seder, a feast layered in song and lyric of the Exodus. Did I want to go?

"*Oy,*" I said. "A seder in Marin, where chic meets *kvetch.*"

A lively crowd gathered, informed and poised. *Seder* recalls bitter oppression in the time of bondage in the land of Egypt. Many opinions rose on oppression and bondage, historic and current, suburban and uptown, general and personal, neurotic and comical. Ah, Jews on Passover. And nobody should be made to feel alone on the subject of oppression.

Two children shared ideas from literature. Two other kids played a horn and piano recital before dinner—jazz, erratically syncopated, dissonant and eerily soothing.

I thought of youth and lakes in winter and summer.

When the recital ended and the kids relaxed, the mother turned to me. "Tell us something."

I shrugged. "I was in St. Louis, visiting family. I try to go every six months. My mother gave me some old photos. They're in the car. I can get them, if you want to see."

"We do!"

"Sixty, seventy years old, some of them."

"Your grandparents?" they presumed.

"No. My old . . . My father was nearly fifty when I was born. Him and his family, mostly." I went to fetch my envelope.

I shared the oilfield photo on top. They passed it carefully. Another guest, Todd, said it felt unique in setting, obviously, but something else about it seemed eerily distant, and he couldn't quite put his finger on it.

I said, "Yes, it was something else."

Mother had added a few, one of the old man in antique football gear—lumpy leather pads and helmet and a funky jersey, like an old Gipper movie.

They laughed, asking if that shot was Halloween.

"No. That's the old man, suited up for life." I told them about the '23-'24 season when he played left guard for the Cleveland Tigers, a farm club for Cleveland. In a three-point stance, he looked at the camera, ready to take it out, the grin in first-phase power at twenty-three.

Another surprise shot showed the old man in wrestling trunks, ready to rumble.

"Your father was a professional wrestler?" Todd asked. Todd had two kids. One had played trumpet. The other aspired to writing. Todd was about my age and sold insurance.

"Yes. It was different then."

"Different?" Todd asked. "How so?"

"More impact. Much closer to what they appeared to be."

He smiled, still polite, and the brisket was served. Todd said, "I wanted to be a wrestler but got into insurance. It's similar."

We laughed, remembering what we wanted to be, and talk got sparse, with much to eat, opinions on hold, except for compliments to the cook.

Later that night, in my room at my friend's place back in the city, I pulled the curtain to see the alley. It seemed bigger than alleys used to be, the far wall friendlier, its windows reflecting city lights. Time had come around, the aft to the fore of it, to a familiar place where a highball made sense. I hung my clothes, straightened my stuff, found bourbon in the liquor cabinet and poured one over, with a splash. I sat at the table for another look in the envelope.

The wrestling picture was from '32 or '35 and explained Mother's discomfort back in Hoosierville, where professional wrestling was far from the high-paying showbiz it became. And what a long shot from the refinement she tried to impart. The pro ranks then were a bunch of tough guys grappling for a few bucks—guys who could take a fall and throw another punch on the way up. That felt familiar. Those guys mixed it up, engaging life on rigorous terms. He kept up with those guys for years.

As a kid in Southern Indiana, I had the other kids amazed to hear that I'd gone back to the locker room at the Channel 7 Wrestling place, that I actually shook hands with Johnny Valentine, the champ, master of the elbow smash.

Just over in the next row of lockers, Rip Hawk brooded, ready to fight his pants, one leg at a time. Rip Hawk was an original bad guy with a platinum blond flattop and black eyebrows. He looked up and smiled, seeing us. He stood to ruffle my hair. I didn't mind. He threw a soft punch at my shoulder and advised. "Don't take any shit, kid. Just don't take any shit."

Down at the end: Bobo Brazil, the Black giant whose hands could cover a man's head and hold it in place, just so, for the Cocobutt. Bobo Brazil leaned way down to my level, where he shook my hand and blinked, "How do you do, Sir?"

And way over in a corner, alone with a single locker that looked and felt removed in every way: Dick the Bruiser, the original wrestling psychopath who bled buckets and kept coming on, who threw three chairs instead of one, who never seemed entirely out of character. He didn't ruffle a kid's hair or shake hands or anything. But he didn't ignore the old man either. He stood and faced off, grunted, nodded and said, "Hey, Leon. How's it going?"

Dick the Bruiser!

The old man nodded on mutual respect. They shook hands.

He liked staying in touch with that action, like it was purer and easier to take than what waited outside.

The old man was thick as a redwood in the wrestling shot, the big grin in love with the moment, fists clenched, energy coming on, like a camera click was the only time left before the knuckles hit your nose.

EPILOGUE

THE ICE KING is a midlife memoir, commemorating the thirtieth anniversary of the old man's—my father's—funeral, as that revisit helped to resolve unfortunate events of the past and to help shape a brighter future. The action carries to 1992 and on to '99.

People tend to preserve iconic images, indelible impressions and lasting influence. For me, Professor Natural of *Zap Comix* fame summarized best in an eight-frame encounter, opening on a sink filled with dirty dishes and buzzing flies. Professor Natural enters, sees, rolls up sleeves, washes the dishes and stacks them in the rack, where they sparkle. No more flies.

He turns to the camera in the last frame, and his talk bubble says, "Don't mean shit."

Most things don't. I never found the long-lost manuscript but realized in '02 or '03 that only a pussy would bemoan a lost manuscript for so many years, especially having found the first hundred twenty-five pages. Getting a story going is the hardest part, and this one was up to cruising speed. It got revised and rewritten, different from its original version and better. Marty

Shepard at The Permanent Press nominated *In a Sweet Magnolia Time* for a Pulitzer Prize, which also didn't mean shit, with NY interests scrumming for position and payout. Permanent was way out on Long Island, where Marty knew the score but said, "Hey. It's on us if we don't put it out there."

Flossie's son checked out at ninety-two on a pharmacy miscue and the wrong antibiotic. Or some shit.

The Devilment perished about the same age from Covid.

Sissy and her husband moved to a newer, bigger house in a much better suburb.

Brother got a new massage chair and an electric car for the many miles back and forth daily to assisted living, where Mother moved to at ninety-seven.

Mother became Old Mom, alert and demanding to the end at a hundred and one, nearly a hundred and two. Semiannual visits helped us recall and prioritize yet again. I pondered wrong and right for years with regard to filial devotion, in both natural and toxic measure. Perspective led to clarity, subjective maybe, but comfortable and accurate from here.

Better yet, Old Mom basked in listening to readings from my work, either past or in progress. She often dozed off those last few years in front of the TV or talking to others, but never during a reading. An author is sensitive to who's paying attention. Eyes wide, ears perked, she would nod, remembering or realizing. She wasn't exactly the Ice Queen but was the best mother ever.

Oh, yes, she loved this one.

About the Author

Robert Wintner has authored twelve novels, three memoirs, four story collections and five reef photo books. He crossed two continents on motorcycles, sailed four of the seven seas, dove tropical reefs around the world and rose from ashes to success in a place *Forbes* magazine called the most difficult business arena in America. Profiled in a dozen metro daily papers, interviewed on a hundred radio shows, he declined Leno when asked to arrive in mask, fins and snorkel. He is committed to style, story, entertainment and lasting value intact. He's Executive Producer of *The Dark Hobby*, an award-winning feature film exposing the aquarium trade's devastating impact.

Robert Wintner is the nom de plume of Snorkel Bob, Hawaii's reef outfitter, known for quality and hygiene in trying times. He lives on Maui with Anita, Cookie the dog, Yoyo, Tootsie, Rocky, Buck, Inez and Coco the cats, and Elizabeth the chicken.

Made in the USA
Columbia, SC
03 June 2023

17483884R00152